WHAT WOULD PLATO THINK?

Aadamsmedia

Adams Media
An Imprint of Simon & Schuster, Inc.
100 Technology Center Drive
Stoughton, Massachusetts 02072

First Adams Media hardcover edition
November 2022

ADAMS MEDIA and colophon are
trademarks of Simon & Schuster.

For information about special
discounts for bulk purchases,
please contact Simon & Schuster
Special Sales at 1-866-506-1949 or
business@simonandschuster.com.

The Simon & Schuster Speakers Bureau
can bring authors to your live event.
For more information or to book an
event contact the Simon & Schuster
Speakers Bureau at 1-866-248-3049
or visit our website at
www.simonspeakers.com.

Interior design by Colleen Cunningham
Interior layout by Michelle Kelly
Images © 123RF; depositphotos.com

Manufactured in China

10 9 8 7 6 5 4 3 2 1

Library of Congress Cataloging-in-
Publication Data
Names: Wittkower, D.E., 1977– author.
Title: What would Plato think? / D.E.
Wittkower, PhD.
Description: Stoughton, Massachusetts:
Adams Media, 2022.
Identifiers: LCCN 2022006125 | ISBN
9781507219683 (hc)
Subjects: LCSH:
Philosophy--Miscellanea.
Classification: LCC BD31 .W58 2022 |
DDC 100--dc23/eng/20220325
LC record available at https://lccn.loc
.gov/2022006125

ISBN 978-1-5072-1968-3

Contains material adapted from
the following title published by
Adams Media, an Imprint of Simon
& Schuster, Inc.: *The Philosopher's
Book of Questions & Answers* by D.E.
Wittkower, PhD, copyright © 2013,
ISBN 978-1-4405-5886-3.

CONTENTS

INTRODUCTION

Does money buy happiness?
Why is there evil?
Should you do bad things for the greater good?

*Questions like these have fascinated people and the world's philosophers for centuries; questions that seek an answer to what we are, what we believe, and **why** things are the way they are.*

The word *philosophy* means "love of wisdom," and this captures well what philosophy is and why it is of constant relevance to us. Philosophy doesn't just seek knowledge; it tries to find the meaning and relevance of that knowledge. It seeks an understanding of not just what we are and what the world is, but also what difference it makes and how we can know what is possible for us to know (and what is not).

What Would Plato Think? will show you how the wisdom of the ancients and the speculation of contemporary philosophers can support your own examination of philosophical questions—questions for which there are no clear and unambiguous answers, but which are of such great importance to us that we can't give up on asking and trying to answer them.

Each entry in the book has two parts: On the first page you'll find a philosophical discussion of a particular issue and on the next, some questions that explore that issue. There are several ways to work through the book. One is to try a daily routine: Sit down in the morning and explore the philosophical discussion over coffee, think about it during the day, and make time to write your answers to the questions in the evening. On the other hand, you may want to sit down to explore an entry at a single sitting. No matter what approach you take, the book will work best if you go through the entries in order—they build from one to the next to develop different aspects of each topic.

The ideas and arguments you'll encounter here will challenge you. Some will challenge your beliefs and push you to consider things in a new light. Others will challenge you to live up to your own beliefs and to make a new commitment to your values and your vision of your best self and the best world we can create together. Above all, though, working through these questions should be fun, interesting, and informative—not because you'll be learning about the views of philosophers, but because these views will give you new ways to learn more about yourself and about the world!

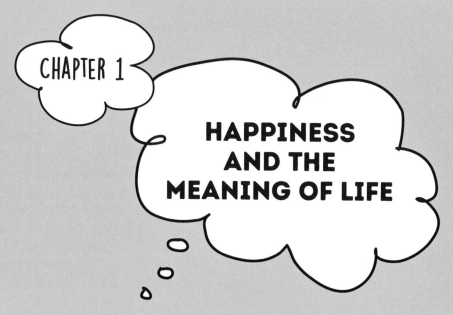

CHAPTER 1

HAPPINESS AND THE MEANING OF LIFE

The good life was a central concern to the ancient Greeks, and asking what kind of life was best led them to consider virtue, freedom, pleasure, and happiness. In medieval philosophy, these concerns shifted to considerations of sin and salvation. In modern philosophy—and for philosophers the "modern" period starts in the 1600s, with René Descartes often used as a dividing line—the question becomes not "How should one live?" but "How should one act?" and the question of the good life becomes secondary to questions of moral behavior and ethical choices. Still later, especially along with the rise of religious skepticism, agnosticism, and atheism, the question of the meaning of life became pressing.

While that's the shape of the general trend, these questions are obviously connected, and philosophers (and others) have had all of these concerns in all of these different periods. We won't go through them in any historical order. As you'll see, though, once we start pulling on a particular thread, the fabric will bunch up, showing how intertwined these concerns and questions are.

CAN YOU MAKE YOURSELF HAPPY?

Happiness is a confusing, fleeting thing. If we devote our lives to our own self-interests and benefits, we typically end up fairly miserable and alone, and the most selfless and giving people seem to be at least among the happiest of people. This is what philosophers call "the paradox of hedonism": If you pursue nothing but your own happiness, you can't reach it.

This idea is typically traced back to the ancient Greek philosopher Aristotle (384–322 B.C.E.), and he has a way out of the dilemma as well. Aristotle thought our proper goal in life was *eudaimonia*, which is often translated as "happiness" but is better understood as "flourishing." To flourish is to realize your *arete*, which is often translated as "virtues" but more literally means "the best possibilities of your nature." Once we put all this in everyday language, it sounds familiar: Aristotle said that your goal should be *self-actualization*, which is being your best self and living your best life #blessed.

Knowing what the "self" is that we're supposed to actualize is the problem. When we follow lower parts of ourselves that we have in common with other living things—pride, anger, desire, and simple hunger—we act hedonistically and selfishly and don't end up happy or flourishing. When we follow higher and distinctively human parts of ourselves, like reason and the search for truth, we end up being honest and caring and courageous, and realizing that best self by living our best life; that's what makes us happy.

Happiness can only be reached indirectly: You end up happiest when you just try to do the right thing, and when you try to make yourself happy, you often enough end up feeling worse. But if Aristotle's right, we can work toward *flourishing* directly, and that will tend to make us happy.

Aristotle's view is that your character is formed by habits, and to be your best self, you just have to do what your best self would do until it comes naturally to you. Think of a couple of your best habits to support yourself and others—like kindness, respect, responsiveness, acceptance, and so on. How did you develop or cultivate those habits?

Think of a couple of bad habits of thought or action that you have, either toward yourself or toward others. What would you like to be doing instead that would be healthier and more supportive? Come up with a plan of daily visualizations and affirmations and weekly activities that you can start doing to help you move toward becoming that better self.

CAN MONEY BUY HAPPINESS?

What do you want money for? Maybe you want to travel to marvelous places, climb Mount Everest, or help the poor. But can you achieve similar goals and have similar experiences with the resources available to you right now?

The ancient Greek philosopher Epicurus (341–270 B.C.E.) was a hedonist and held that the good life and happiness were found by pursuing pleasure and avoiding pain. How did he avoid the paradox of hedonism? By saying that the problem isn't pursuing pleasure, it's pursuing pleasure in a crude and thoughtless way.

When we think of hedonism, we tend to think of things like expensive meals and fancy houses and cars. Rare and hard-to-obtain pleasures that come with wealth may be great, but think of everything you have to sacrifice to get them! Plus, when we enjoy great luxury, or enjoy being a great philanthropist, we soon develop expensive tastes. Once our happiness is bound up in becoming and remaining wealthy, fear and uncertainty begin to dominate our lives.

Life becomes more and more about keeping and getting more of the resources that we've made our happiness depend on, and less about doing things that actually make us happy.

To be happy and peaceful, Epicurus advocated living simply, and not getting too involved in wealth, politics, or even physical desires like those for sex or food. As often happens, his doctrine has become twisted over time, and today "Epicurean" refers to a taste for very sophisticated and refined foods. For a true sense of Epicurus's view of the good life, cook turnip chunks with lentils in water until done. Don't add anything else, not even salt. Eat it with someone you enjoy spending time with, and then go for a walk together. Let this recipe make Epicurus's argument; let it show you that making things more sophisticated or fancy doesn't necessarily make them better.

If you had ten times your wealth and ten times your income, what would you do that you can't do now?

What's a version of that activity that you could do right now with your current resources?

Is the current version ten times less meaningful, important, or enjoyable than the activity you would do with more money? Why or why not?

IS ALL HAPPINESS EQUALLY GOOD?

John Stuart Mill (1806–1873), a British utilitarian and political philosopher, thought that the right action was always the one that provided the greatest good for the greatest number. But how do you figure out what is good for someone—or for anyone? Does everyone have the same idea of happiness? Are some ways of being happy "better" than others?

Mill thought that the only proof that something is good in life is that people, in fact, seek it out—and since people choose to live in lots of different ways, there must be lots of different ways to live a good life! But what about people who don't care about art or culture, or encountering new ideas, or being socially aware? What about people who just want to eat chips and watch bad TV and avoid thinking? Can their "happiness" really be considered equal to the happiness of a decent person of refined taste who cares for others?

To fix the problem, Mill added a criterion to what counts as part of happiness. Not everyone is able to appreciate a quiet evening spent with a good book, but those who can tend to prefer it to watching trashy TV (although mindless TV can have a place in a good life too). That means that watching trashy TV is actually a lesser happiness than reading, even though there are plenty of people who'd pick trashy TV every time.

As Mill put it in *Utilitarianism*: "It is better to be a human being dissatisfied than a pig satisfied; better to be Socrates dissatisfied than a fool satisfied. And if the fool, or the pig, are of a different opinion, it is because they only know their own side of the question. The other party to the comparison knows both sides."

What's one of your guilty pleasures—a "bad" TV program, secret romance novel habit, or something similar?

If you feel guilty about it, why do you keep doing it?

On the other hand, if it's something you enjoy, and it's not immoral, why do you feel guilty about it to begin with?

Everyone has guilty pleasures. What if we all made them central to our lives instead of hiding them away? What would change? Would our world be a better place or a worse one?

IS HAPPINESS EVEN THE GOAL?

Is happiness really what you're aiming for in life? Most of us would say yes, and yet every day we make decisions that actually make our lives harder in the day-to-day reality of living—for example, training for a marathon or taking the hardest classes in school. Why do you choose to do hard things? Do struggles make life better? Is the pursuit of happiness really all you are after?

As a culture, we've gotten into the habit of acting like everything we do is about trying to be happy, but we actually care about plenty of other things as well, and in fact we find those things a lot more meaningful than happiness.

In his book *Thus Spake Zarathustra*, German philosopher Friedrich Nietzsche (1844–1900) gives us a vision of a possible pathetic future of humanity: the Last Man. The Last Man seeks only happiness, and is free from the toil and turmoil of questioning and striving and seeking. (I have no evidence that the movie *WALL-E* was based on Nietzsche's idea of the Last Man, though the parallels are striking.) But it is not too late, Nietzsche tells us through his character Zarathustra: We still have enough chaos within us to give birth to a dancing star!

Study after study on parenting and happiness finds that having kids makes us feel less self-satisfaction and less happiness on a day-to-day basis. When confronted with this empirical data, parents usually insist "It'll be worth it!" and "I'll be happier in the end!" Why don't we just recognize that happiness isn't the only reason we do things, and certainly isn't the only reason things are worth doing? How empty and worthless the world would be if our own private enjoyment were the only reason to get up in the morning!

Make a short list of the things you've chosen to do in life and to care about that have increased the suffering, struggle, and trials in your life.

For what reason or reasons did you make these choices?

Would you make the same choices if you could do it over?

IS MEANING EVEN THE GOAL?

What difference will your life make in the world? Will it have meant anything in the end? Everything we do is taken apart by time. As the Book of Ecclesiastes puts it, "I have seen all the works that are done under the sun; and, behold, all is vanity and a striving after wind." What sort of life is a life worth living if nothing we do seems to make a difference in the end?

French-Algerian absurdist philosopher Albert Camus (1913–1960) adapted an ancient Greek story—the myth of Sisyphus—to force us to confront the meaninglessness of life. Imagine Sisyphus, punished eternally to push a rock up a hill, only to watch it roll back down every time. A more meaningless eternity cannot be imagined. Camus asks us how this is different from our lives. We all struggle and toil to achieve our goals, and whatever we put together is taken apart in time. What we do for ourselves is taken from us by death, but even what we do for others—to care for the sick, help the needy, or advance science and human understanding—is inevitably erased by time.

Camus asks us, though, "Can we imagine Sisyphus happy?" Camus thinks we can. We can imagine Sisyphus taking pleasure in a cool breeze as he descends the hill, and the enjoyment of work and of the body as he puts his shoulder to the rock once more. By imagining Sisyphus happy, he means to show us that just because life amounts to nothing doesn't mean it isn't worth living.

Richard Taylor (1919–2003), an American philosopher, asks us further: What if Sisyphus desired nothing more than to push this rock endlessly? Then he might find not just moments of happiness in his toil; he might find the whole process to be meaningful. What is it to find something meaningful other than to desire to do it? Is this closer to what our lives are like: meaningless in that they amount to little or nothing, but meaningful to us through the process of living itself?

What practical goals do you have in life? Think about family, career, hobbies, and personal passions.

If you achieve these goals, or if you fail, what difference would it make one hundred years after your death? Or one thousand years after?

Does this make you rethink your goals? Why or why not?

WHAT IS FREEDOM WORTH?

Most people would probably make significant sacrifices to be free and independent. But are there some things that are worth more than independence?

Not according to Stoicism, a philosophy very popular in ancient Greece and Rome. It taught that the key to a good life was to identify what was up to you and what was not, and to care only about those things that were up to you. Epictetus (55–135), a Stoic philosopher and freed slave, outlined the meaning and implications of this simple idea in his *Enchiridion* (Handbook), which was kind of an ancient self-help book.

To remain free and in control of your own happiness, you must care only about things that are up to you. "So, you want to compete in the Olympic games?" Epictetus asks. If you say you wish to train hard, push yourself constantly, twist your ankle, eat sand, and, in the end, lose—then you may compete and be free and in control! But if you want to *win*, you are a fool, for this is not up to you, and this desire puts others in control of whether you are able to reach your goals and be happy.

Even your body isn't up to you: Others can make choices about it. There's a story that when Epictetus was still a slave, his master, enraged about some perceived wrong, broke Epictetus's leg. Epictetus did not resist: He knew what happened to his body was not up to him and that caring about it would only deliver control of his life into the hands of others. By deciding not to care for his physical welfare, Epictetus remained entirely free and in control even as he was in chains.

Do you have what it takes to be free? Is it worth it?

We usually regard freedom and self-determination to be central to a good life. When have you sacrificed something else in your life—perhaps in your work life, your love life, or just your way of life—to ensure that you are able to make your own choices and not be dependent on others?

Was this sacrifice worth it? Why?

If not, why not? If so, how much further would you go?

WHY DO WE CHOOSE CONVENIENCE OVER MEANING?

Meaninglessness isn't just an abstract concern tied to death and purpose; we struggle with meaninglessness and tedium on a daily basis. Doing the laundry *again* is a small, quiet sort of existential crisis, but it's one you have to face pretty often. Contemporary American philosopher Albert Borgmann (1937–) thinks more efficient technology plays a role in making our lives feel emptier and more meaningless. The reason why is best shown through contrast with "the old ways."

In the days of woodstoves, the need for warmth gave structure to our days. The hearth was a focal point in the home; its fire gave each family member a role to play: gathering and chopping wood, building the fire, cooking on the stove. The family would huddle around the hearth in the morning, and as the heat expanded through the house each family member would move out to their tasks, but as the cold set in the family would return to the hearth in the evening. Today, on the other hand, with devices like central heat and gas or electric stoves, warmth is provided through a simple switch, and the family and rhythm of the day are no longer structured by the need for warmth. The family may stop meeting for breakfast or dinner, may stay isolated in their rooms, each equally evenly heated at all times. The structure and interdependence that the hearth required of us made our lives connected and meaningful.

More efficient technology demands less of us as users—Borgmann calls it the "device paradigm"—and so it provides less of the structure and purpose that make our lives feel meaningful. The point isn't that we should go back to doing things the old ways, but that as we lose structure from technology we should be careful to build it back in somewhere else. Borgmann thinks that a drive-through hamburger has a place in a well-lived life, but if we only do things the efficient and undemanding way, our lives start feeling empty.

So don't go live off the grid (unless you want to), but cook family meals sometimes at least. Grow a garden, even though you could just buy vegetables in the supermarket. Make some music, even if it's awful, instead of only listening to it!

Even if we find our lives to be meaningful, that certainly doesn't apply to every part of them. What are some of the most meaningless things you're going to have to do today?

Of the activities you listed above, what purposes do they play in your life? Are there more meaningful things you could be doing to serve those purposes instead? For example, could you go for a run through the woods or on the beach instead of putting in time on the treadmill at the gym? Could you go on a "friend date" to hang and run errands together?

DOES WORK MAKE OUR LIVES MEANINGLESS?

You are probably familiar with Karl Marx's (1818–1883) opposition to capitalism, but the German philosopher's reasoning behind this opposition is less well-known. The details can offer insights to all of us living under capitalism, whether or not we wish to see the system end.

Marx believed that what made humans distinct from other animals was our ability to change the world based on our own desires and creative vision. This ability to not just consume, but to also change and create the world, is what he called our "species-being." In his early work, which was more about culture than economics, he outlined several ways that those of us who have to get jobs to survive are alienated from our basic nature, from our species-being. We are alienated because we don't design or choose the things we make; because we make them using tools, techniques, and materials that aren't ours; and because the value of our work, crystallized in the things we make, belongs to someone else. We don't have ownership over the product of our labor, and during our working hours we don't have ownership over ourselves.

Marx says that we sell the most human part of our lives—our creative, productive abilities—which becomes "labor," a necessity and a burden. Then we only feel free outside of working hours, where we concentrate on our lesser, animal needs for consumption and rest. In this way, the worker is alienated from their own humanity: They feel least themselves when they're building and creating, and feel most at home when they are focused on needs and desires that we have in common with animals.

This argument is a lot less compelling today, since the labor movement, inspired in part by this very argument, made wageworkers' lives a lot better than they were in Marx's day, establishing the eight-hour workday and the weekend, abolishing child labor, and creating things like benefits and paid time off for many workers. But the basic dynamic of the thing hasn't changed, and even today, many workers feel this alienation keenly.

In your work life, how much can you choose what you do or how you do it? Could work life be structured to give you more freedom?

What difference does the work you do make in the lives of others? What control do you have over the meaning and impact of your work? If you work for a corporation, how much do you control the meaning and impact of your company?

IS WORK MEANINGFUL AT ALL?

Just as it's said that no one wishes on their deathbed that they had spent more time at the office, so too we might imagine that if we could look back from the end of human history, we wouldn't wish that we as a species had spent more time working. Instead, we tend to think that knowledge, understanding, discovery, togetherness, connection, creativity, art, and beauty make up the meaning of our species, if anything does.

And yet, as German-Jewish philosopher Herbert Marcuse (1898–1979) pointed out, once the labor movement achieved the forty-hour workweek, we didn't push forward to the thirty- or twenty-hour workweek. Why not make thirty hours the standard for full-time, benefits-earning employment? What sacrifices have we made as a people to have faster mobile phones, tougher plastics, and a few more dozens of new streaming shows? What would our lives be like if we spent less time working? What other forms of richness would we have instead?

Marcuse said we built a wartime economy for the war against nature. We connected work and moral worth because we needed to struggle to survive. But we've more than won the war against nature, and yet we keep pushing to produce more, quicker, faster, better—and we've tied moral worth so tightly to productivity that we think it's acceptable to let people die from preventable disease because they can't pay for medicine, or to let people live (and die) on the streets when so many houses are empty. We have, Marcuse thought, a long way to go to figure out how to build an economy for a time of peace.

Assuming you're working full-time, about 35 percent of your waking life during your working years will be spent at work. Are you happy to have your work achievements take up over a third of your life for these years?

Consider how many other people are similarly devoting this portion of their lives to work, and what it all adds up to. Is our standard of living worth a third of our lives? Is this what a third of humanity's hours should amount to?

Assuming for the moment that they are practical possibilities, are you opposed to a universal basic income, universal healthcare, or free housing on moral grounds?

HOW DO WE CHOOSE HOW TO LIVE?

We don't enter the world with a predetermined set of values, we learn them through our life experiences. Most of all, we learn them through our experiences with others.

French existentialist Jean-Paul Sartre (1905–1980) held that one of the most significant elements of belief in atheism was that, if there is no God, then we are on our own to determine what our lives are to be about. The same sort of thing can be said from a religious perspective, though: Those who decide to listen to one religious authority or another, or follow one text or another, still need to make that choice, and do so knowing that the choice brings along with it a specific set of views on values, meaning, and purpose.

Sartre also claimed that, since there is no authority on what life is about except for all of us particular living people, when you decide how to live, you make a claim to all of humanity—you implicitly claim that your kind of life is a kind of life worth living. You claim that your goals are important enough to

expend the hours you have to walk upon the earth pursuing. We do not receive our values, we choose them, even when we happen to choose to believe the things we are brought up believing.

Would you be happy to have the values embodied in your life be the values of humanity? In Sartre's view, there is no source of values other than people's choosing, and so we have not only the freedom to do whatever we wish, but the responsibility to choose on behalf of all others as well.

Reflect back on the things we've talked about throughout this chapter on happiness and the meaning of life. The things you desire, that make you happy, or that you find meaningful—how did you come to hold those values?

Think about how you live your life. Do you embody values, both for happiness and for a meaningful life, that you would hold up to others as an example of a life well lived? If so, how so? If not, what's something you could change?

CHAPTER 2

GOD

The history of European philosophy is tightly bound with the history of Christian theology, so there's an emphasis here on Christian views. I've tried to present things so that these questions and ideas are as valuable as possible for those of you who are not Christians, but some of the issues don't translate well to other views. If you're Jewish or Muslim, most of the issues will apply equally for you; if you're Hindu or Buddhist, it'll be hit-and-miss; if you're agnostic or atheist, well, you'll probably just be playing along. But that's valuable to better understand what it's like to have faith, and to enjoy the intricacies of religious reasoning. I'm not a Christian, and I have a kind of pure enjoyment of St. Thomas Aquinas's writing; pure because I don't have faith in his sources and have little concern for his topics or answers—and yet I enjoy and appreciate the grace and wisdom of his discussion itself.

It might be good to remind you before you start in here that philosophy is about hard-nosed analysis and criticism. Philosophy is not interested in being reassuring, and it is not interested in making you comfortable. It's interested in discovering the truth, and that means being open to the possibility that the truth is horrible.

WHY IS THERE SOMETHING RATHER THAN NOTHING?

Where did all this stuff come from? How did the chain of cause and effect get started? It seems like change and matter need to come from somewhere. It's unsatisfying to just say that everything's always been around and been in motion, since, well, how can there be an infinite series of effects without some cause to start everything off? Unless we say that there is some kind of "unmoved mover" to get things going, we just have to throw up our hands. Even the "Big Bang" theory doesn't resolve the issue. Why did it "bang"? Where did the thing that "banged" come from? These questions are the basis for what's called the cosmological proof of God's existence. Different versions have been given by different philosophers, with the most famous probably being the versions from Aristotle and René Descartes (1596–1650).

Even though plenty of philosophers thought the "cosmological proof" proved God's existence, it doesn't really. If it's true that "everything's just always been here" and "things have always been moving" aren't good answers—and even if we can't explain the universe without a "first cause"—should we really expect to be able to understand the origin of the universe, or to be so sure that just because human reason says there must be a beginning that it must be so in reality? Even the answer that "God did it" just puts off the cosmological question: We might ask, then, where did God come from? If we assert that God is *sui generis*—that He made Himself by Himself—that's really just as uninformative as saying that the universe made itself by itself.

Whatever we believe, we should have humility about it. Because whatever we believe, it doesn't really answer the question, and it sure seems like nothing ever will.

No, seriously: Why is there something rather than nothing?

Things are happening right now, caused by things that just happened just before the things happening now. And those things must have been caused by something before them, and so on. Does there have to be some kind of first cause that isn't itself caused? Or is it possible that there is no beginning? Or is this a false choice?

If the truth is something beyond our comprehension, does that mean the answer to the previous questions is "both"? Or "neither"? Or something else?

IS THERE A DESIGNER?

English philosopher William Paley (1743–1805) created the famous "watchmaker analogy" as a kind of teleological argument for God's existence—"teleological" in that it is an argument based on the idea of a purpose (from the Greek *telos*).

Paley asked his reader to imagine finding a watch out in the wilderness. He said you couldn't possibly imagine it had always been there, along with the rocks and dirt! Its intricate parts and clearly intentional design imply that someone must have *made* it, and it must have gotten lost there at some point. Similarly, Paley argued, the intricate interconnections between species, as well as the complex design of different organs and bodily systems, could not have come together just so in any mindless and unguided process. So, just as there must be a watchmaker to explain the watch, there must be a Creator to explain nature! There are similar "intelligent design" arguments around today.

It's interesting to see what this argument does and does not establish. These arguments are often used to argue for a Christian conception of creation, but they are just as compatible with any kind of intelligent designer—a flying spaghetti monster, for example. The teleological argument also doesn't establish that evolutionary biology and other sciences won't explain the complexity of design, given time. After all, most theists believe that God works mostly through natural processes rather than miracles, so God's design could possibly be realized through scientifically describable natural forces.

But is science able to explain everything? Maybe. Maybe not. We're a long way from finding out. But whether or not you believe in a Designer, you're better off not using it as an explanation for anything. To say "God did it" only halts inquiry into nature, where we might be able to figure out how things happened—and if you think that this scientifically discoverable natural history is also an expression of God's will, that should probably make it *even more* interesting!

Paley's argument looks like it might be an "argument from ignorance," which is a kind of logical fallacy that basically says, "You can't explain X, therefore X can't be the case." Is it fair to say that the argument is basically "You can't explain how natural selection created the eye or the human brain, therefore God did it instead"?

On the other side of the argument, is it fair to say that it's an argument from ignorance to say "You can't explain how God created humans, therefore it was natural selection"?

The previous entry, Why Is There Something Rather Than Nothing?, said that whatever we believe about the origin of the universe, we should have some humility about it. Should we have the same humility here, or is this a different sort of situation?

WHY IS THERE EVIL?

Now that we've talked a bit about proofs for God's existence, let's look in on a proof against. Here's how it goes:

1. If God is all-powerful, and
2. If God is all-knowing, and
3. If God is entirely good, then therefore, all things are good!

However,

4. Evil exists, so therefore, one of the premises must be wrong.

This argument, best known as "the problem of evil," doesn't claim to prove that some God doesn't exist, only that a God of the sort that most monotheists believe in doesn't exist. But, just like the proofs of God's existence that we looked at earlier, this proof against God's existence doesn't work as well as philosophers who've advanced it seem to think.

Christian philosophers have responded to the problem of evil without departing from a traditional Judeo-Christian understanding of God. The most famous of these is the "free-will defense,"

which says that evil enters the world through human choice, and free will is so important to God that He allows evil for its sake, since God wants more than anything for us to know the Good and choose the Good freely.

Another interesting Christian response is to simply deny that evil exists. St. Augustine (354–430), a North African philosopher, claimed that what we call evil is simply the absence of good, just like how darkness is not a real thing, but only the absence of light. He asked, "What happens to a physical wound or sickness when you are healed?" Does it flutter away from your body to a new host? Of course not; it simply disappears, showing that the injury was not a real thing, but only an absence of health. In the same way, evil is not real; it is only the absence of good. We fall into evil and suffering because God made us from nothing, and when we move away from God's goodness, we tend to return to nothing.

Do you agree with all the listed premises for the "problem of evil"? There are lots of people who respond to the problem of evil by rejecting one of the premises. What if God isn't all-powerful? Is God still God if He is limited in power or is opposed by an evil power that He can't always defeat?

What about the second premise? Is God still God if He can't make all things good because he doesn't know everything or isn't aware of everything that's happening?

What about the third premise? Is God still God if He isn't entirely good?

IS OUR SUFFERING WORTH IT?

Another possible response to the problem of evil is to claim that God allows evil because suffering is necessary for human development. Without the negative, it's claimed, we cannot appreciate the positive, and some elements of human greatness can only be achieved through suffering, strife, and loss.

Many have put forth versions of this "theodicy," or justification of God. Among the earliest is St. Irenaeus (d. 202), and among the most famous is the German philosopher Gottfried Leibniz (1646–1716). The basic idea is that even though there is evil and suffering, this is still the best of all possible worlds. This might be because the evil in the world is outweighed by the good that is made possible through that evil. It's also been argued that it wouldn't have been logically possible for God to have created a world without these flaws—for example, that any being other than God will be subject to errors in knowledge and moral failings, simply because they are finite.

Others have argued against this view. For example, the German philosopher Arthur Schopenhauer (1788–1860) argued that you could see immediately that the good in the world does not always outweigh the evil simply by comparing "the respective feelings of two animals, one of which is engaged in eating the other." William R. Jones (1933–2012) put forth a fascinating challenge to this theodicy in his 1973 book *Is God a White Racist?* He asked whether we can defend the idea that all injustice and suffering will be redeemed when we consider the history of racially discriminatory violence and suffering.

What justification can be given for God's inaction in the face of the enslavement of Black people or the Nazi's genocide of Jewish people? What greater good could outweigh this suffering?

What great trials have you faced in life? Have they changed you for the better or for the worse? If you don't think you've faced any great trials, think about someone who has, and imagine their answer.

What are some examples of kinds of suffering that almost always improve the people who undergo them?

What kinds of suffering are unlikely to improve those who undergo them? Is there such a thing as a pure loss—suffering unredeemed or unredeemable by growth and progress?

CAN SUFFERING BE GOD'S WILL?

The suffering of innocent individuals, like the suffering of peoples and races, provides a difficult challenge to any theodicy. This is one among many philosophical themes explored in *The Plague*, a novel by the Nobel Prize–winning French-Algerian absurdist philosopher Albert Camus (1913–1960).

In the story, an Algerian town suffers a rare outbreak of bubonic plague, which kills much of the population before the town's doctors are able to develop a cure. Father Paneloux, a Jesuit priest, gives a sermon early on in the epidemic where he draws on the image of a threshing floor. It is through the violence of the plague, he claims, that God separates the wheat from the chaff, the virtuous from the sinners.

But Paneloux finds that he can no longer believe that suffering can always be justified as a punishment or a trial after watching a child suffer a slow and painful death from the illness. He asks himself instead whether the suffering of an innocent can be made up for by the eternal bliss of heaven. If it can be, he reasons, then Jesus's suffering on the cross becomes meaningless, because it is only a moment of pain outweighed by an eternity of happiness. Jesus's suffering cannot serve as a means of human redemption if it is not truly a sacrifice. Paneloux finds he can't brush away the suffering of a child by asserting that all will be made right in the next world. Instead, Camus wrote, Father Paneloux "would stay at the foot of the wall, faithful to the excruciation symbolized by the cross, face-to-face with the suffering of a child."

For a moment at least, adopt the idea that suffering is sometimes a divine punishment for sin. Can this explain the suffering of terminally ill infants and children, or of animals burned alive in a forest fire? What other explanation can you offer?

How should we differentiate deserved from undeserved punishment in the suffering of others?

How should we separate deserved from undeserved punishment in our own suffering?

CAN FAITH BE JUSTIFIED?

In this chapter, we began with attempts to prove that God exists (and saw that they didn't work), moved to arguments that a God who is good and in control *can't* exist (and saw that they didn't work), and then turned to cases that require the faithful to affirm God's will in the face of complete incomprehension of how His will could be justified. Is faith then purely an arbitrary and indefensible choice?

Considerably more can be said in favor of religious faith according to American philosopher William James (1842–1910). In his 1896 essay "The Will to Believe," he argued that there are some kinds of things that we are justified in believing in the absence of sufficient evidence. For example, you might not know whether your neighbor likes you. If you withhold judgment until you know for sure, you'll be reticent and reserved, and they'll be less inclined to like you if they don't already and less likely to continue liking you if they already do. On the other hand, if you go ahead and just believe that your neighbor likes you, you will be more friendly and outgoing and your belief will tend to make it true.

In another example, if you are considering marrying but are not sure that your partner will live up to your hopes, your doubt will poison and end the relationship. Only through believing in your partner's goodness are you able to have a life together in which you are able to find out whether they are the wonderful person you believe them to be.

Religious faith, according to James, works the same way. Belief in the goodness of the world tends to make the world good, and belief in religion opens us up to the kinds of experiences that justify faith, which the doubter may never experience. This doesn't mean that we all necessarily *ought* to have religious faith or that faith is correct, but James claimed that belief in a God that is good and in the goodness of the world can be justified by its effects, even in the absence of sufficient evidence.

Do you think God exists or not, and why? What evidence do you have in favor of your position? How did you come by this evidence?

What does your faith in the existence or non-existence of God tell you about how to act and what we owe each other?

IF GOD TOLD YOU TO DO SOME-THING IMMORAL, WOULD YOU?

This question makes an assumption you might want to reject. Is it even possible for God to tell you to do something immoral? If God is good, how could God tell you to do something evil? Or, alternately, if God tells you to do it, doesn't that make it the right thing to do?

This is what's called "The Euthyphro Dilemma," named for Plato's dialogue "The Euthyphro." In the dialogue, Socrates (469–399 B.C.E.) confronts an earnest man named Euthyphro about his beliefs about piety. Piety, in Euthyphro's view, is doing what the gods love. But why, asks Socrates, do the gods love some things rather than others? Because those things are holy, answers Euthyphro. This brings up several troubling questions:

- If it is pious to do what the gods love, and the gods love what is holy, then why not just say that it's pious to do what is holy, and leave the gods out of the whole discussion?
- Alternately, if it isn't holiness that makes the pious action

pious, then couldn't the gods love what is unholy—and wouldn't that, then, be what is pious?

In the context of modern Christianity, the question is whether good and evil are based on God's will, or whether God's will is based on good and evil. Either position appears heretical. If "good" means nothing but "what God says to do," and "evil" means nothing but "what God says not to do"—a view called "divine command theory"— then God could say that murder is right, and it would be…and that sure doesn't seem right. And worse yet, how can we claim that God is good, if "good" just means "whatever God says"? On the other hand, if God is telling us to do what is good because God is good, then good and evil exist independently of God, and God is just offering advice about a moral system that God is Himself subject to!

If God told you to do something immoral, would you do it?

Think of a religious text that you know pretty well. Are there any parts where good deities seem to do or ask others to do bad things? What do you make of that?

DO YOU NEED THE WORD OF GOD TO BE A GOOD PERSON?

In many faiths, this question isn't a big issue. In Hinduism and Buddhism, for example, you can be a good person without any particular knowledge about this or that deity. You just have to be compassionate, care for others, stand for what's right, and so on. We can all pretty well figure out that stuff on our own, even though moral and religious texts might be helpful along the way. Some Christians think it's a big deal though, and some theologians have claimed that "Revealed Law"—the word of God, contained in the Bible, sent to guide humanity—is necessary for salvation. It seems a bit unfair to others, though, and the question of the fate of the "righteous heathens," like the good and moral people born before Jesus, has been an issue of debate. Would God really condemn them to Hell because they didn't have access to divine text that hadn't yet been written?

One way of mitigating this seeming divine injustice is the idea of "Natural Law." The idea is that God's will can be determined by looking to God's creation, where we can see implicitly the rules for moral conduct that are stated explicitly in God's word. Through use of reason alone, we can determine, for example, that we ought to treat others just as we would like others to treat us, and indeed it seems like every culture and religion has its own version of the Golden Rule.

In this view, even our bodies can instruct us in God's will through Natural Law. For example, philosopher St. Thomas Aquinas (1225–1274) argued in *On Kingship* that we could tell that God intended us to live in community with one another and under a government because He created us without tough hides or sharp claws. It's a bit undignified, but effective: We learn to live along with others, to be citizens and subjects, because our other choice is to die cold and alone or get eaten by animals.

Think again about a religious text that you know pretty well. What sorts of guidance does it contain that people wouldn't follow unless they read and believed that text?

This guidance—is it moral guidance? If not, what kind of guidance is it?

Does whether or not someone follows this guidance seem like the right kind of thing for them to be condemned for or redeemed by, according to the overall view of divine justice in the text?

ARE BODILY DESIRES BAD?

For creatures said to be created in the image of God, we are awfully messy, hairy, smelly, and desirous things, aren't we? If this idea of Natural Law is going to hold up, we need to have some explanation for why—if nature is supposed to be a guide to the same moral law contained in Revealed Law (in the Christian context, the word of God contained in the Christian Bible)—our bodily natures seem to drive us into all kinds of coveting and licentiousness.

Both Augustine and Aquinas were influenced by Aristotle's understanding of the human as a "rational animal." In this view, we are animals first, and rationality—the soul, in the Christian sense—is added later. (This is why the Church regarded abortion as morally acceptable until the nineteenth century—through the first trimester, the fetus was thought to be just an animal, with no soul.) So, we have our animal nature as well as our higher nature, and that means that we retain some biological imperatives and urges proper to animals, as well

as those distinctively proper to humans. The pleasure we take in the body is natural and proper to our animal nature, and contributes to its well-being. The pleasures of the table drive us to maintain our bodily health, which we need for our individual survival, and sexual pleasure drives us to procreate, which we need for the continuation of humanity. Our nature, though, should also teach us that reason, which humans alone have, is more important than the body, which we have in common with all animals; so we should see (as did Aristotle and Plato) that it is right that our desires be kept in check rather than given free rein. But those urges are not sinful in themselves—they are proper to our animal nature. The sin is when we act like mere animals when we are something more, and when we make our higher, rational self the servant of our lower, animal self rather than the other way around.

Based on this idea of Natural Law, why might it be that other bodily attributes sometimes seem to drive us toward less moral behavior? Why would God make us this way?

Do you consider any of your bodily urges immoral? If not, why do you think others might? If so, what do you do to control these urges?

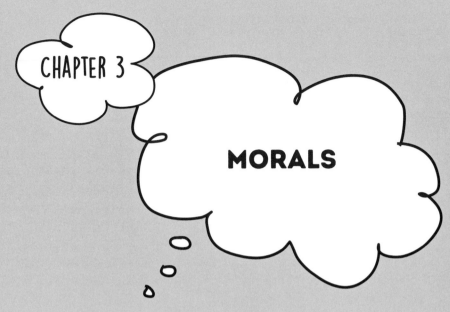

CHAPTER 3

MORALS

How should we act? On what basis do we decide on our courses of action? What do we mean when we say something is "right" or "wrong" in a moral sense? These are among the many questions that we will most definitely *not* answer by the end of this chapter. We'll take a pretty good look at things, though, taking a quick trip through duties and intentions, utilitarianism, virtue ethics, ethics of care, and a couple of issues in religious morality.

Questions in ethical theory, for the most part, have less to do with *what* to believe about right and wrong than they do with *why* we believe what we believe. Any decent ethical theory will recognize the complexity of our lives and give us troubling or ambiguous answers to questions about how to act in troubling or ambiguous circumstances. To put differences between one theory and another into sharp contrast, philosophers sometimes turn to contrived, artificial, or extreme made-up examples. Sometimes these "thought experiments" help us to clarify our views like they're supposed to, but sometimes they make complicated issues seem far too simple. You'll see what I mean.

ARE GOOD INTENTIONS ENOUGH?

If you do something bad because you're trying to harm others, that definitely seems to indicate that you're a bad person. But what if you think you're doing the right thing but harm others anyway?

Immanuel Kant (1724–1804) thought morality was entirely about our intentions. It makes sense that someone as religious as Kant would believe so: If morality is about the contents of the heart, then we are entirely in control of whether we are moral or immoral, and that helps to justify the idea that God will reward or punish us according to our moral worth. But Kant's argument for the idea has nothing to do with his faith. He argued that having a good will toward others is the only truly and purely good thing that we can have. Even virtues like cleverness and conviction can become evil when held by those with bad intentions! So whether you are a good person comes down to whether you have good will toward others.

But surely those who do bad things often have what they think are good intentions. So Kant

worked out an objective test for whether our intentions really *are* good: Your intentions are good if you're trying to act according to intentions that could be adopted by everyone else as well, and which, if adopted by everybody, would result in a world that we'd like to live in. What this does, basically, is identify when you are making an exception for yourself when you expect everybody else to play by the rules. Do you think a world where nobody trusts each other because everyone lies all the time would be bad? Yeah, well, then don't lie. Ever.

Can good people do bad things? Give some examples.

When a good person does something that turns out badly or has unintended harmful results, does this make the person less good or less moral? Why?

Don't lie, ever? Really? Do you think there are times when the right thing to do is maybe to do something admittedly wrong, for the greater good?

IS LYING EVER OKAY?

As you saw in the previous entry, just telling yourself or believing that you have good intentions isn't enough according to Kant: The action you intend to take has to be universalizable. But this focus on just the action itself seems really rigid and inflexible, and it seems like it just entirely ignores the *consequences* of the action. Can't the end justify the means at least sometimes?

Many have taken this to be a fatal flaw in Kant's theory, but Kant was well aware of this seemingly unacceptable implication of his view, and considered it more a feature than a bug. Philosophers will often provide what's typically called the "murderer at the door" case as if it's a real "gotcha!" moment, without explaining (or often even realizing) that it's Kant's own example or providing his solution to the case!

Imagine that someone comes to your door intending to murder your friend, who is hiding in your house. Lying is wrong for Kant, because it can't be universalized: If everybody deceived others when it was helpful, deception would become impossible, because no one would believe anyone anymore to begin with.

So you can't lie to the murderer at the door, even to save your friend, which seems like you need to get your priorities straight. But Kant said that you can't know the intentions or the heart of this stranger at the door; you only know they're angry and maybe violent. If you lie, you treat them as if they will always and only be a murderer. (This is why even calling this case "the murderer at the door" goes against Kant's point!)

By telling them the truth instead, you confront them with their own intentions and give them the chance to change, grow, and redeem themselves. Kant thought that everybody is owed respect as moral agents, meaning that everybody deserves to be treated as someone who, even if they're a bad person right now, could *become* a good person. So where Kant seems rigid and judgmental—it's always wrong to lie!—what he was really doing was telling you that being moral means radical love and acceptance, and that we should confront immoral people with their own actions by leaving the door open to the better person they could become.

Describe a lie or half-truth that you've told that you think was clearly justifiable.

What good outcomes did you close off by lying? What could the truth have changed if things had gone well?

What kinds of circumstances or conditions do you think justify lies? What needs to be at stake in order to justify a lie—or, alternately, how trivial does something have to be before you are justified in lying about it?

CAN THE ENDS JUSTIFY THE MEANS?

Kant's theory about the basis of morality is not the only one around. The "utilitarian" theory of John Stuart Mill is the one that may seem the most commonsense to most of us today, even though the term "utilitarianism" makes it sound technical and obscure. Utilitarianism is the idea that we ought to act to maximize utility, where "utility" just refers to anything anyone has a use for. So maximizing utility just means making the world a better place for everyone.

What good is a theory that just seems…obvious? Well, it tells us that *consequences* matter, not intentions, and that we can decide what's morally right by comparing possible actions and "doing the math" to figure out which one makes things more beneficial for more people. So, it's pretty useful in helping to make decisions when we're not sure what to do. But even though trying to create the greatest good for the greatest number generally fits pretty well with our ideas of right and wrong, it also may seem to put us in some weird spots.

Imagine that you promised to pay some kids down the street to rake and mow your lawn. When they're done, you look at the money you're about to pay them and realize that it would make more of a difference in people's lives if you gave it to charity. Should you go ahead and tell the kids that you decided it'd be better not to pay them?

Mill anticipated cases like this. He said that we need to think about long-term effects and social effects, not just the immediate impact on those directly affected by our actions. If you break promises, you undermine the trust and cooperation that our society depends upon. You might be helping some people, but you're not not teaching those kids good values. We care about telling the truth because honesty is usually a great way of getting to the greatest good for the greatest number!

So, moral rules like honesty are important for the utilitarian, same as they are for Kant. But for the utilitarian, moral rules are only important because they tend to maximize benefits for people, so, unlike Kant, the utilitarian thinks there can be some exceptions. How far do the scales have to tip, though, to make breaking a promise okay?

Imagine you answer an ad for someone who wants you to be executor of their will. They say they don't trust their family to do it. When they die and you look through the will, you understand why: Their entire estate is to be given to a neo-Nazi group. Would you be justified in "misplacing" the will in a nearby fireplace?

Imagine a relative of yours—say, your aunt—is dying and asks you to leave as her bequest a large sum of money to another relative, who already happens to be well-off. You promise to do so, and your aunt dies. Nobody else knows about this money or her request. Would you be justified in donating the money to a homeless shelter instead?

SHOULD YOU PULL THE LEVER?

Imagine these two scenarios:

- You see a trolley rolling toward five people who have been tied to the track. You don't have any way of stopping the trolley, but you can switch it to a different track. There's only one person tied to that alternate track. Should you throw the switch?
- There's no switch, but this time, you do have something nearby that could stop the trolley: a very fat man. If you push him onto the track, the trolley would derail after hitting him, and save the five people tied to the track. Should you push him?

These are troubling questions, and if you really think about what it would be like to make the call, it might be hard to imagine throwing the switch (or the fat man) even if you're convinced that it's the right thing to do.

The reason why ethicists have played around with these examples—the first originally comes from English philosopher Philippa Foot (1920–2010), and the second from American philosopher Judith Jarvis Thomson (1929–2020)—is that "thought experiments" like these help us to isolate our moral intuitions and understand why we believe what we believe.

We're much more likely to find it acceptable to switch tracks than to throw the fat man on the rails, even though the losses and gains are the same in both cases. But why? Some think it's because in the first case we're just reacting to a situation in progress, and all six people are already inside the situation, whereas in the second case we're adding someone uninvolved into the situation, which makes us feel more responsible. But how important should our feeling of responsibility be, compared to saving lives? Another theory is that in the second case we're actively intending someone's death, whereas in the first, the death of the single person on the other track is just a kind of side effect of saving the five.

Real-life circumstances are much more uncertain and complicated than thought experiments, and taking harmful action is very difficult to justify, even in circumstances that seem most in its favor.

Imagine that a terrorist group has claimed that they will set off a bomb that will kill at least five people. You have a member of the group in custody, but they refuse to talk. Should you resort to torture if doing so will get you information that will allow you to stop the attack? Why or why not?

Let's revisit that thought experiment, but this time imagine what it would actually be like. The terrorists say there's a bomb, but the whole thing could be fake. If it's real and you get information from this person, you might not be able to stop the attack anyway. Also, keep in mind that people being tortured who don't have the information the torturer wants will make up stuff to get the torture to stop. How does this change things? Given these changes, when and how would you say thought experiments are useful?

HOW MUCH DO ANIMALS COUNT IN THE GREATER GOOD?

If we adopt the utilitarian view that the right action is the one that produces the greatest good for the greatest number, then we just need to do a kind of cost-benefit analysis to figure out how best to act. For each possible choice, we add up the happiness of each individual benefited and then subtract the suffering of each individual harmed. We can then take whichever action has the greatest net benefit (or, if all our options are bad, whichever action has the least net loss). But who counts as an individual? Do birds count, for example? Do we weigh their happiness as heavily as that of a person?

Australian philosopher Peter Singer (1946–) thinks we can account for this using his "preference utilitarianism." What counts for him are preferences that can either be met or denied. This allows him to set up a kind of moral spectrum among animals. People have all kinds of preferences—not just suffering and pleasure, but plans for the future, desires, intellectual enjoyment, furthering our causes and values in the world, and so on.

Other animals, like dogs and cats, can't have, for example, political causes or favorite pastimes, and this limits the range of preferences they can have. Still other creatures, like clams or insects, have very limited preferences, perhaps limited to preferring not to suffer.

For Singer, animals count to the extent that they are able to have preferences, and this lets us compare the limited (but often serious) preferences of nonhuman animals against the less limited (but often trivial) preferences of humans. As soon as we set up any such grounds for inter-species comparison, Singer thinks we should immediately realize that eating veal and foie gras is obviously unacceptable, that cage-free eggs are certainly worth the extra couple dollars, and that animals need to be included in all sorts of public policy choices.

Imagine you're in charge of making the final choice about where to put up a dam to create a reservoir for a municipal water supply. One valley is used occasionally by hikers. Another is almost never visited but is the nesting ground of a particular bird species, which would be displaced by the reservoir. How do you weigh the inconvenience to the hikers against that to the birds? Does the birds' happiness have moral weight?

Do you buy cage-free or free-range eggs? What decision-making process do you use in the grocery store to decide whether to spend more to get food that is more humane or more environmentally sustainable?

Let's revisit that example, but in the form of a thought experiment. Imagine someone hands you a chicken and says they'll pay you $5 to break one of its toes. Does this thought experiment bring the right issues about factory farming of eggs into focus, or is it misleading or distracting?

HOW DO YOU BECOME YOUR BEST SELF?

Modern ethical theory concentrates on how to act, but the ancient Greeks were more concerned with who you should *be*; your character rather than your choices. We still think about this issue today, of course, and philosophers continue to think about these questions of character, most often by returning to Aristotle's theory of virtues, or *arete*. You may remember some of his take on virtues from the discussion about his view on happiness in Chapter 1.

Having a virtuous character, being your best self, means that you have a habit and inclination to do virtuous things. Being courageous, for example, means you're likely to do the right thing even when it's dangerous or frightening. But how do you become virtuous? By getting into the habit of making good choices. We become the kind of person who enjoys a healthy way of life, for example, by making healthy choices even when we don't want to. Eventually, it starts to come naturally.

We can use reason to help develop good habits and virtuous character. The principle of "moderation in all things" or "the golden mean" helps us to figure out what courage is by looking at the middle ground between the extremes of cowardice and recklessness, or to work out a healthy relationship to food by avoiding the extremes of overindulgence and self-hating abstinence as well.

Very often, though, the path to our best selves comes not by abstract reasoning, but through a moral exemplar—a role model that we admire and seek to emulate. How much have the character traits you value in yourself been brought about by careful thought, and how much by emotional connections to people who represented those traits for you? Even when we become disillusioned about a role model, as too often happens, we owe a lot to the people we thought others were, and we can still seek to embody the virtues we thought we saw in them.

Make a short list of people you admired when you were growing up. Try to think of people who inspired you at different ages.

What about these people made them important to you?

How do you think your attachment to each of them influenced your development?

CAN IMPARTIALITY BE IMMORAL?

Modern ethical theories like Kantianism and utilitarianism focus on justice and impartiality. While this focus leads us well in many ways and helps us explain a lot about why we believe what we believe about right and wrong, in some situations impartiality can actually seem wrong. Imagine, for example, that there are two people trapped in a burning building and one of them is your child. Would a good parent approach the situation objectively? If you chose to save the stranger and leave your child behind, since objectively that was the action most likely to save a life, wouldn't your child feel betrayed, and wouldn't you feel guilty? There's a moral dimension to personal relationships that theories of justice and impartiality struggle to explain.

A more recent ethical theory, feminist ethics of care, responds to this problem. Feminist theorists noted that the ethics of justice and impartiality were grounded in public life and policy choice—traditionally male domains—while ignoring the traditionally feminine ethical realms of home and family. When we focus instead on home and family, we see that personal relationships have distinctive and different moral elements, where we commit to one another, put people we care about first, and approach each other through love rather than by thinking about what's "fair."

Ethics of care isn't "women's ethics"; it's not that women have "care" and men have "justice." We all participate in both. But the way we have overvalued the stereotypically male domains of work and government and undervalued the stereotypically female domains of friendship, hearth, and home led ethicists to overemphasize justice and fail to appreciate care. Working out the proper balance of justice and care, and in which situations one or the other ought to determine our actions, is not an easy matter, but it's a good starting point to recognize that impartiality by itself is clearly not enough to stand alone as the basis for a moral life.

Imagine you're judging a talent show for elementary school students, and your child is competing. Is there any reasonable way you could justify choosing your child as the winner if you believe another child put on a better performance?

Now imagine that a fire breaks out. There's not enough time to get every child to safety. Are you justified in rescuing your child rather than another child who is nearer to you and whom you are more likely to be able to save? After all, that child has parents who love her too. Is your child more important than theirs?

What about buying your child a new toy when the same money could be spent funding vaccinations that could save a child's life in Africa? Is this form of favoritism moral?

WHEN SHOULD YOU TURN THE OTHER CHEEK AND WHEN SHOULD YOU TAKE A STAND?

Jesus's claim in the Christian Bible that you should "turn the other cheek" is often understood as an ethics of nonresistance. Let go and let God! But Walter Wink (1935–2012), a Christian theologian, gave a compelling but too-little-known account of Jesus's Sermon on the Mount that provides an understanding of the elements of Christian ethics that's in line with nonviolent resistance, and similar to the ideals and practices of Martin Luther King Jr. and the American civil rights movement.

Wink points out that, then as today, striking someone with the back of your hand expressed contempt and superiority. If you think about the physical act of turning your left cheek to face someone who has struck you on the right, you can see that, if one of the Jews listening to Jesus did so when struck by a Roman, the Roman would be forced to either use his left hand (which was considered improper) or strike them with a fist or open hand instead. Far from being submissive, turning the other cheek forces the Roman to attack the Jew as an equal instead of using the backhand, and makes a strong political claim of equality and worth without resorting to violence or retaliation.

Jesus also advised to "give the shirt off your back" in a time when being naked in public was shameful. Debt holders were legally allowed to demand cloaks from those unable to pay. By advising Jews to give their shirts as well, Wink claimed, Jesus showed how they could demonstrate that they had been insulted and oppressed by purposefully debasing themselves. In the same way, people in occupied territories could be forced by Romans to carry their packs for a mile, but only a mile. By "walking an extra mile," as Jesus advised, Jews could take control of the situation and, through overcompliance, implicate the soldier in breaking the law!

In this understanding, Jesus didn't teach passivity at all, but passive resistance. What has been interpreted as a moral teaching of acceptance and nonresistance was really a political teaching about insisting on equality and standing against injustice.

Think about "turning the other cheek" as it is usually understood, refusing to meet violence with violence. Does turning the other cheek mean allowing oppression to continue?

Choosing on your own to overlook offenses against you seems noble. But what about attacks against others? Should you "turn the other cheek" when you see a wrong done to someone else?

What about actions or words against you that affect others indirectly? If you are a minority, would you turn the other cheek when someone insults you for your race, religion, or identity? How do you draw the line between nonviolent forgiveness and failing to do your part in standing up to abuse and hatred that also harms your sisters and brothers?

CHAPTER 4

JUSTICE

Questions about morality are closely connected to questions of justice. It may be fair to say that questions of justice are moral questions pursued at the level of policy. This includes policy questions about what people deserve and how to distribute limited resources, but it also includes policy *about policy*—how we should make choices, and what sorts of limits should be placed on the choices that can be made.

This chapter starts with questions about structures common to today's representative democracies. The topics have an American emphasis, but the issues should be recognizable and entirely relevant to anyone living in a democratic republic. From there we'll turn to what philosophers often call "distributive justice," or justice in allocation of resources, where we'll look at topics like bias, rights to profit, property rights, and taxation.

There was a time when we had arguments and debates about the fundamental issues behind markets and property rights, but we rarely do today. Instead, we tend to just assume that the property rights we're used to must be good and must be justifiable somehow, because they've been around for a while. Once you open up these issues and start asking questions you don't usually ask, you might find out you're less certain of what you believe than you thought.

WHO SHOULD BE IN CHARGE?

To live together, we need to make choices that balance the needs and desires of some against those of others. Even most anarchists recognize this need—their view is that these systems of power and control should be momentary, limited, and local, not that we can live together without ever having someone making tough calls. Given this broad agreement that we need "deciders in chief," who should they be?

Plato used the famous analogy of the "ship of state" to address this. He asked us to imagine a ship at sea in need of a captain. Those fighting to be the one to take control have all sorts of reasons to want to be captain. Some seek to steer the ship because they believe they know what's best; others seek control because they want to feel important, or because they are power-hungry. Now imagine that you look away from the fray and notice someone off to the side, unconcerned, staring at the sky. Here, Plato said, is the true ship captain: a useless stargazer! Only he knows the stars, which are the right basis for steering the ship—only he knows how to use the polestar to find north, to guide the ship along its route and then back to port.

For the same reasons, he claimed, the philosophers should rule the state. Like the stargazer is interested only in discovering what is constant and what changes among the stars, the philosophers are interested only in finding what is constant, what is true and real, and what changes and is temporary and contingent. They care most about truth and finding out the reality of things, which should be the proper basis for making decisions, not power or pride or self-interest. Those who seek power do not deserve it, and those who deserve it do not seek it. But should we, as Plato thought, make philosophers kings, and make all others subject to their rule? For those of us who believe in democracy, Plato's problem is real and serious, but his solution is hard to accept.

Running for political office is a disruptive, difficult, expensive process. How much do you think politicians are motivated by idealism, and how much by a desire for control?

There are a great many people—economists, policy analysts, scholars of poverty, and so on—who are experts on issues of great concern for the nation. Why aren't they in office?

What kind of people do you want in office, and how could we get them there? Why would they be more effective than those who are currently in office?

CAN A DEMOCRACY AVOID FALLING INTO MOB RULE?

Historically, the idea of democracy has been a hard sell. Put the people in charge of themselves? *Have you seen the people?* One fundamental problem with democracy is the risk of "faction"—the risk that a larger group will vote for their self-interest in a way that seriously harms a smaller group. Under majority rule, the minority is subject to the will of the majority—and if the majority doesn't care about the minority, the minority can't use majority rule to protect itself!

In *The Federalist Papers*, written during public debate about whether to ratify the Constitution of the United States, Alexander Hamilton (1755–1804), James Madison (1751–1836), and John Jay (1745–1829) explained how the US Constitution was written to try to fix or at least mitigate this problem. Federalist 10 said that "no man is allowed to be a judge in his own cause," and that a democratic system needs to be sure that factions, in the form of voting blocs acting on mere self-interest, can't just take over. The solution, according to James Madison in Federalist 10, is *representative* democracy in a democratic *republic*. By having

choices made by a "congress" of representatives, the public will can be "refined and enlarged" by this small group of public-minded patriots, since they will represent the interests of the voters, but when there are conflicts they'll weigh them against the greater good of the nation. Federalist 63 describes how differences between the House and the Senate strike a similar balance. The House is subject to frequent elections so that its members are forced to remain true to the direct and stated will of the people. Senators, on the other hand, are elected for a longer term so they are able to make choices that might be unpopular but will pay off in the end.

In today's media environment, however, we have detailed day-by-day coverage of what happens in Congress, and elections have spread out so that representatives are almost constantly in "campaign mode." This is clearly good for transparency and responsiveness but bad for making good but unpopular choices. Thus we have begun to see the return of the problems of "mob rule" and faction that our representative republican structure was meant to solve.

In the simplest form of direct democracy, we would simply vote on everything. In this system, would the many poor simply vote to take and distribute the wealth of the rich? Would the majority simply vote to remove rights from racial or other minorities? Do you think direct democracy would lead to greater justice or greater injustice? Why?

In a representative democracy, we sometimes speak of elected officials as "employees" of those they represent, whose job is simply to bring their public's opinions into legislation. Does this bring up the same "mob rule" problems as direct democracy might?

WHY HAVE WE SETTLED FOR CONSUMER DEMOCRACY?

The Federalist entrusted representatives to place local and factional needs and desires into a wider context, and to moderate current passions by long-term goals. Another possibility is that we, the people, could refine and enlarge our views in this way *on our own*. Are we so mired in self-interest that we can't have reasonable, careful discussion with one another and come to agreements on our own rather than delegating these hard choices to representatives? It might seem pretty hopeless in our current political environment, but it hasn't always been this way, and it doesn't have to stay this way.

The German philosopher Jürgen Habermas (1929–) has done historical work showing how a "public sphere"—a cultural space where people from many different backgrounds came together to openly debate policy, current events, art, and all sorts of topics—emerged in eighteenth-century Europe along with the rise of coffeehouses and newspapers. People had the time, information, and communicative opportunities to engage in thoughtful public debate about the politics of the day, and it became possible for there to be such a thing as "public opinion," rather than merely individual views or official state perspectives.

Things have gone downhill since then. Today we have fallen away from a "deliberative democracy," where we engage in public debate and decision-making, to a "consumer democracy," where we as citizens simply choose between the options presented by those supported by major parties who are wealthy enough to run for office. The media supports and enables this situation by focusing on the horse race and party-line pugilism of politics rather than promoting thoughtful public discussion and real debate. Even preferential voting wouldn't change this, but breaking up the two-party duopoly would at least open things up to more options and ideas. The road to a political culture in which we all engage in discussion about issues and policy rather than candidates and party platforms will be a long one.

Imagine you're against all wars, or opposed to any corporate influence in government. Who can you vote for? What can you do to get your view represented?

Imagine, like many Catholics, that you are in favor of social programs that help the poor, but against war, and against abortion rights. Which party can you call your own? How can you decide which lives to support through your vote and which to abandon?

In preferential or instant-runoff voting, you rank your choices for office. If your first choice doesn't win, your vote goes to your second choice, so that voting for a "minor party" candidate isn't "throwing your vote away." How much of a difference would this make for you? Why do you suppose we don't use preferential voting?

SHOULD WE JUST CHOOSE OUR LEADERS AT RANDOM?

One thing that makes philosophy distinctive is its willingness to consider any possibility, and to call into question even things that seem natural and commonsense, to see whether they are merely something we're used to or if they can stand on their own merits. Sometimes, in desperation, we think we'd get better politicians by picking names at random from the phone book. And, well, why not?

This is the model we use for jury duty. We have the idea that justice is often best served by a jury of people chosen at random, rather than leaving guilt or innocence to experts or "career jurists" or something. In ancient Athens, not just juries but most governmental offices were filled by lottery, and some contemporary writers, like Ernest Callenbach (1929–2012), have discussed the possibility of returning to this seemingly radical idea.

How radical is the idea, really? If we believe in democratic ideals, shouldn't we want choices to be made by regular people? Of course, on the face of it, we might imagine people just legislating based on their own limited knowledge and prejudices, but the checks and balances could help to ensure that the closed-mindedness of a few can't take over, and more responsible citizen-legislators could draw on the knowledge and research of experts, just like juries choose based on expert evidence and argumentation.

Elections support party politics rather than open debate and deliberation, and the expense of elections means that poor people are unlikely to gain office. The need for campaign donations gives undue influence to the interests of corporations and wealthy individuals. Would we be better off without having elections at all? Are elections, on the whole, good or bad for democracy?

Recent estimates are that about 8 percent of adults in the United States have a net worth of a million dollars or more, but that 52 percent of the members of Congress are millionaires. What effect, if any, do you think this has on our elected representatives' ability to represent us?

Founders of the United States intended political representation to be a kind of public service that citizens would make for a time, then return to their regular lives, and Americans today are suspicious of "career politicians." Would things be improved if we limited all elected officials to a single term of office? Why or why not?

WHY IS BIAS SO HARD TO GET RID OF?

In a 2004 study, University of Chicago professor Marianne Bertrand and Harvard professor Sendhil Mullainathan found that identical resumes sent to job ads in Boston and Chicago got 50 percent more calls for interviews if the names at the top were Emily and Greg than if they were Lakisha and Jamal. This is just one of many studies that show that racial and gender biases still exist in our society even though almost nobody thinks that racism and sexism are acceptable. Given the empirical fact that discrimination is happening, if it's not because of racists doing racist stuff, why is this still happening?

One reason is confirmation bias. We internalize cultural images and associations: We see Latino actors as drug dealers in crime dramas; the woman of the house is already there when the sitcom kids get home from school; all Indian characters work in IT. These internalized images condition how we interpret others, even though we usually don't believe that they represent anything real or meaningful. The mind, like everything else, tends to follow the path of least resistance, and stereotypes pave the way for confirmation bias. You can feel this at work for yourself by taking an Implicit Association Test—Harvard's Project Implicit has some very good ones online.

Maybe most telling is that those subject to discrimination internalize stereotypes as implicit bias too! Rev. Jesse Jackson admitted to having implicit bias when he said, "There is nothing more painful to me at this stage in my life than to walk down the street and hear footsteps and start thinking about robbery—then look around and see somebody white and feel relieved." Implicit bias is like a virus, not a choice. When you're exposed to racial and gender bias, it tries to take hold, and it'll use you to spread itself.

Since implicit bias is unconscious, and since it changes how you perceive yourself and others, the best thing you can do to avoid being "contagious" is to try to become conscious of common biases so that you can notice them when they come up. For example, if you find yourself thinking a woman is bossy or demanding, ask whether you'd think a man saying the same things was confident or assertive.

Talk to a friend who is a different race than you. Ask them what their race has meant to them practically, and how they believe it has influenced how they have been perceived and treated. Don't talk about your own view of it, or your own experience, just listen. What part of your friend's experiences was most surprising to you?

How has your experience of the social meaning of your race been different from your friend's? What has been easier for you and what has been more difficult?

How has others' perception of your gender influenced how they think about and treat you? If you could change one aspect of those biases, stereotypes, or assumptions, what would you change?

IS CAPITALISM JUSTIFIABLE?

Most of the world today lives under capitalism, and when something is really common and widespread, it starts to seem "natural" to us, and we don't spend a lot of time questioning it or thinking about arguments in its favor. When people do argue in favor of capitalism, though, most often they seem to use some version of the idea of the "Invisible Hand."

The basic idea is that in a transparent and open market, free competition based on profit motive will set prices in a way that uses natural and human resources in a maximally efficient way, resulting in an improved standard of living that benefits everyone. A business that charges too much will be undercut by a competitor. If a production process is inefficient, a competitor will figure out a better way so it can sell the product for less and take over the market. By acting in our self-interest in this competitive environment, the argument goes, we end up with better results for everyone than we would have if we planned things out and tried to help people on purpose.

The Scottish moral and economic philosopher Adam Smith (1723–1790) first formulated the idea, but important parts of his view get lost today. For one thing, he meant this action of the market to be a protection against selfishness, whereas today it is given as a *justification* of selfishness! Also, today we tend to talk about profits as something capitalists have a right to take, but for Smith, profits were justified only as a generally useful means to create a prosperous and just society.

Smith's vision of what that society would look like is also different from what we'd expect. In his *Theory of Moral Sentiments*, he argued that the rich would be "led by an invisible hand to make nearly the same distribution of the necessaries of life, which would have been made, had the earth been divided into equal portions among all its inhabitants." Given that he thought the Invisible Hand would create near equality of wealth, if Adam Smith saw the inequality of our society, our rampant selfishness, and the massive profits of corporations, he would regard capitalism as a failed experiment, in this regard at least.

We typically recognize that we can achieve more by cooperating with others, and working together. What sense does it make that production in our society is based instead on competition?

The way we live today makes us dependent on others for food, water, housing, and energy. Why do we allow those providing goods necessary for life to "skim off the top"? Why not provide these goods on a nonprofit basis?

We say it takes money to make money, and surely having a greater initial investment makes success and market dominance more likely. Does that mean that the rich, on the whole, get richer, and the poor generally stay poor? If so, is that a good way to run a society?

ARE PROPERTY RIGHTS ABSOLUTE?

The moral justification of capitalism is sometimes also traced back to English philosopher John Locke (1632–1704). Unlike Adam Smith, who argued for free-market competition based on the greater good for all of society, Locke argued that we have a God-given individual right to our property. If Locke is right, then it seems like whether capitalism is best for society is irrelevant—it's our right to do what we want with our property, and that's the bottom line.

Locke argued that although the world was given to humanity in common, we were given our own bodies individually. This is why we can control our bodies with our minds, and, try as we might, we can't control anything else that way. Based on this, he argued that whatever we mix our bodies with—by expending the hours of our lives improving it through our labor—becomes rightly our sole property, so long as we leave enough of nature for others to do the same. So if you make some clothes from fabric, or even just pick some berries out in the forest, you've mixed your labor with it, and it becomes your right to keep or sell it, and to profit from your work.

There's been some question of what a Lockean view implies about eminent domain laws, which force landowners to sell land when necessary for the public good. The Lockean view assumes that if you didn't own anything, you could just go out and find a spot nobody was using and till the soil. Today, it's not clear that there's "enough and as good" of raw nature for us to go out and improve through our labor. The fact that almost the entire planet is already owned by someone makes an absolute right to property more questionable, and the idea of eminent domain seems more necessary.

There are also debates about what Lockean theory means for taxation. If we're going to have public goods and works (roads, for example), it seems only fair that everyone should help pay for them. But if our right to property is God-given, then how can it be just to force anyone to give up any of their property?

What are the limits of our property rights? Is it acceptable to use eminent domain to force people to sell their homes at fair prices if the land is needed for social utility, like building a new airport? What about if it's for economic growth, like building a new factory or sports stadium?

If we have a right to our property, then taxes require moral justification. If you thought it was okay to force the sale of property for an airport, does that also justify taxes for social goods like military defense or public healthcare? How much of the tax burden should fall on workers, how much on owners of businesses and investments, and how much on businesses themselves?

IS PASSIVE INCOME JUSTIFIABLE?

If we agree with Locke that property rights are based on labor, how is "passive income" from owning businesses or properties justifiable? It's tempting to say that the labor bound up in the wealth used to buy businesses and properties continues to generate a right to some of the profits generated with this wealth, but Locke would want to say that's owed to the people actually doing the work! A better answer is to appeal to the greater good, and say that paying passive income to useless owners is worth it because we need to keep economic capital in motion to keep the system going—but then we have to ask whether the greater good is served by structures that tend to help the rich get richer while keeping the poor poor, and whether there is another way to provide liquidity that reduces inequality instead of increasing it.

This issue isn't really a topic of debate today, but it certainly has been in the past. Charging interest on loans was particularly controversial, and used to be called "usury." St. Thomas Aquinas wrote that "to take usury for money lent is unjust in itself, because this is to sell what does not exist, and this evidently leads to inequality which is contrary to justice." The money has its own value, printed on its face. The argument is that to charge more than that amount for it is to charge both for the object and its use, as if we sold someone a bottle of wine but demanded an additional payment if the buyer decided to drink it.

John Calvin (1509–1564), the Protestant reformer, thought that there were fair ways of charging interest, but that for the most part "the practice of usury and the killing of men" are justly placed "in the same rank of criminality, for the object of this class of people is to suck the blood of other men," and "men should not cruelly oppress the poor, who ought rather to receive sympathy and compassion."

Do you think it's okay to charge interest on a loan? If so, explain why.

On the assumption that there is some justification for charging interest, are we justified in charging more to the poor and desperate? If our property rights are absolute, can we justify laws against predatory lending—payday loans at very high rates, for example?

Based on your answers to the previous questions, consider making an investment. Are you entitled to profits from someone else's work because you supplied start-up funding? Given that these profits come from someone else's labor, isn't the laborer entitled to keep them? If not, how much of the profits are you entitled to, and why?

SHOULD COMPANIES ONLY CARE ABOUT PROFIT?

Nobel Prize–winning economist Milton Friedman (1912–2006) argued that public companies are the legal property of shareholders and therefore should be run based on shareholders' interests alone—and he said it's reasonable to assume that the shareholders' only interest is profits. Under this "shareholder theory" of corporate social responsibility, the corporation has an obligation to (legally) maximize profits no matter what. Any compromise of profitability for whatever purpose—helping the environment, paying employees well, donating to social causes—he compared to a form of taxation without representation, claiming that the CEO is basically taking someone else's money and spending it on whatever he thinks is important, which is almost a kind of theft.

Friedman's view has been hugely influential among many people in business and a great many legislators as well, despite the fact that a large part of the public finds it immoral. Friedman's arguments for it are awful too. It's not at all reasonable to think that shareholders wouldn't trade slightly slower growth for better environmental or labor practices.

Shareholders don't own the company in any way that would justify the claims about taxation and theft either: They *hold a share* of its profits. Under an LLC (limited liability corporation) structure, shareholders can't be held liable when the company is found guilty of fraud or negligence, specifically because they don't own the company and aren't in charge of what it does. Why should the company be solely responsible to investors when they are not held responsible for what it does on their behalf?

The stakeholder theory is the other main perspective on corporate social responsibility, and it holds that businesses should consider the welfare of all stakeholders, not just the shareholders. The overall idea is that if businesses are dependent on their natural and social environment, then it makes sense that businesses would have an obligation to help maintain a prosperous society, a healthy educated workforce, and a business environment where the public generally trusts corporations. After all, we can have a society without businesses, but there can't be businesses without a society.

Ford Motor Company produced the Pinto, which had a design flaw that made the car prone to catch on fire, especially when in rear-end collisions. Ford determined that the cost of a recall, plus the $11 per car it would take to repair the issue, was greater than the likely cost of lawsuits brought by those injured and the families of those killed in these preventable accidents, and decided not to do the recall. Did they make the right call? Why or why not?

If it's profitable to do so, should a public company pollute as much and as often as is legally allowed? Why or why not?

Given that public companies have an obligation to give investors a return on their investments, what kinds of public interests are sufficient reasons to sacrifice profits for?

IS TAXATION THEFT?

Taxes have been in the background of many of the previous entries, and it's time for us to face the issue head-on. If we have property rights over our income, or have the right to transfer property, or set our own prices in a free market, how is it okay for the government to force us to give them a cut? There's a word for taking someone's property without their consent: theft. Is taxation just theft in disguise?

A classic answer is to say that taxation is part of the "social contract," part of the ground rules that everybody needs to play by to make our society work, but this rings a little hollow. None of us ever got a real choice about whether or not to agree to the social contract, and besides, can't a social contract be unjust? Some societies are more fair than others, but it seems like saying "it's part of the social contract" doesn't really explain anything, since it could be said equally well in any society.

American philosopher John Rawls (1921–2002) came up with a thought experiment to figure out which social contracts are just and which are unjust. Since we never get the chance to negotiate and consent to a social contract, he asked what kind

of social contract you *would* agree to if you had had the chance. To make sure you're agreeing to the whole contract, not just the part of it that applies to you, you have to imagine that you have a "veil of ignorance" and don't know your social class, race, gender, sexual orientation, or anything else. What kinds of social supports, public goods, and distribution of wealth and opportunity would you negotiate for?

Rawls said you might start with a safe bet, where everybody has equal rights and opportunities. That way you won't be in a bad spot no matter who you turn out to be! But in a society without *some* inequality, people don't see hard work and innovation pay off, and that means that there's likely to be less prosperity overall. If you add in some inequality, even though there are now some people with more wealth and opportunity and some with less, even the worst-off are doing better than they were in a completely equal society. That's an even better bet! And from here we can say for sure that a careful, rational person behind the veil of ignorance would consent to a social contract that allows just as much inequality as continues to help even the least among us, but not more than that.

So Rawls said we can figure out which social contracts are fair by imagining what someone would agree to if they didn't know who they were, and things we all would definitely want in there include universal basic rights as well as access to the resources you'd need to be able to work and better yourself even if you turn out to be on the less-advantaged end of things when you take off the veil. And to provide that to everybody, and to make sure that we don't let inequality get out of control, Rawls said we would need progressive taxation.

Some people say they shouldn't have to pay taxes to fund public schools since they don't have kids, or their kids go to private school. What if public schools were only supported by parents whose children attended them?

Imagine someone saying they shouldn't have to pay taxes to fund the Fire Department since their house is not on fire. What if the Fire Department was only supported by people whose houses were or at some time had been on fire? Is this a fair comparison with the previous question? What are the relevant differences, and what difference do they make?

HOW MUCH SHOULD YOU GIVE TO CHARITY?

Rawls's justification of using taxes to provide social services is clever and insightful, but even if you agree with it and see how it works conceptually, it'll never change that in actual fact paying taxes is not a choice. It would still be better if we all just chose to help one another!—or, if at least enough of us chose to donate and volunteer. But what obligation do people have to give away their money or time to fix problems that they didn't cause and might have nothing to do with? And what is "enough" help to those in need?

Peter Singer, a contemporary Australian ethicist, has pursued this issue very effectively in journal articles, book chapters, and an excellent article published in *The New York Times Magazine* called "The Singer Solution to World Poverty." Singer asks you to imagine that you've parked your car on some tracks and gone for a walk. You see a train coming and a child tied to the tracks. If you do nothing, the child dies, but there's a switch you can throw to divert the train so that it will destroy your car instead.

(That's right, it's another trolley problem, like the one in Chapter 3!) What kind of monster wouldn't throw the switch? And yet, if we imagine the child is in Bangladesh instead of on the train tracks, and the threat to her life is disease or famine instead of a train, then we seem to have no problem keeping the car and letting her die.

It's an ingenious thought experiment. You're not responsible for the child on the tracks. You don't owe her anything, and she has no right to your help. But even so, would you really choose your car over her life? If not, then maybe our choices about charity have less to do with our values and more to do with how much suffering we are sheltered from and choose to ignore.

You might not be convinced, but you probably agree that it's the right choice to give up some things sometimes if doing so is easy and can greatly improve or even save someone's life. If so, how do you figure out how often is often enough and how much is enough to give? Where and how do you draw the line?

Singer says: "Whatever money you're spending on luxuries, not necessities, should be given away." That's probably a lot more than you were thinking. What could you say to explain why he's wrong (if he is)?

CHAPTER 5

HUMAN NATURE

When we think about the dignity and value of humanity—our reason, logic, morality, humane care, understanding, expansive vision, and spirituality—it seems an insult and affront that our bodies should be made out of meat. Worse yet, we're sweaty and squishy and smelly, and have irrational urges to rub against one another (but only in private, out of shame). "Man," as Arthur Schopenhauer put it, "is a burlesque of what he should be."

And yet, of course, the mind is the meat, at least in some sense. We are our bodies, and yet we are not only our biology. We are animals, but unusual ones who have transcended our animality (maybe). What parts of us are nature, and what parts are nurture?

ARE WE JUST ANIMALS IN THE END?

Diogenes the Cynic (412–323 B.C.E.)—in the Greek, that means "Diogenes the Dog"—thought that even back in ancient Greece, human society had made things far more complicated than they needed to be. The Greek view that the mind or the rational soul was the distinctive and real part of us was mistaken in his view: We may be rational, but we are also animals, and we shouldn't pretend we're not.

Diogenes was known as "the dog" because he lived according to this belief. He slept in a large broken clay pot among the dogs in the street, like an animal. He kept few possessions: a cloak that he also used as a blanket, a cup to drink from, and a bag for food. At some point though, he saw a child drink from a stream using a cupped hand, so he threw away his cup too.

He once carried a lantern through the marketplace at midday, explaining "I am looking for a man." This is often retold as "looking for an honest man," but the meaning is the same: He was illustrating the futility of finding anyone honest about what it is to be human, and claiming that everyone else was in the dark and not even seeking the truth.

Although he used unusual and shocking methods of propounding his views about human vanity and the actual simplicity of human needs, he was recognized as a wise man. As his army moved through Greece, Alexander the Great (356–323 B.C.E.) sought out Diogenes. Alexander found him sleeping in a ditch on the side of a road and said that he had heard of Diogenes's wisdom and would give him anything he desired. As Alexander stood over him, Diogenes replied, "Stand out of my sun." By asking the most powerful man in his world for something he couldn't control, the *sun*, but something granted freely to the lowliest animals, Diogenes demonstrated his view that Alexander's power and wealth were irrelevant to our real needs and desires. Alexander left him in the ditch and is said to have commented, "If I were not Alexander the Great, I should wish to be Diogenes the Dog."

Our biological drives are very simple, even if we include social-biological drives like seeking comfort, friendship, and play (games, music, dancing, and so on). How did things get so complicated?

What would a society directed purely to satisfying these basic interests look like?

Would you like to live there? Wouldn't it be possible for you to "drop out" of society, join a commune, and live a simpler, more natural life? Why (unless you do live on a commune) haven't you done so?

WHY DO WE CARE ABOUT OTHERS?

As Australian philosopher J.L. Mackie (1917–1981) pointed out in a famous article, "The Law of the Jungle," evolutionary survival of the fittest doesn't happen on an individual level but on a genetic level. So although there is individual competition for mates and food and so forth, a great many species (including our own) compete in their larger environment by banding together. Selfishness might further an individual's interests, but genes that motivate us to look out for one another—an uncle to protect his niece or cousins, for example—are carried forth generation after generation because they create mutual benefits. The willingness to sacrifice your own interests or even your own life may not help *you* survive, but it helps that gene survive, and that's what matters evolutionarily, as Richard Dawkins showed in *The Selfish Gene*.

Consider an example of Dawkins's that Mackie used: Imagine a species of birds who are parasitized by disease-carrying ticks. If each bird only looked after itself, they'd all die, because they can't remove the ticks from the backs of their own heads. So they groom one another. Now imagine a genetic variation that presents itself to be groomed but didn't waste time helping out by grooming others. Those birds would have more offspring and take over the society, and then the ticks would spread and that group of birds would decline or die. Bird groups will do best if they help each other, but also root out and shun the cheaters. This strategy is called "reciprocal altruism": to groom another bird unless you find out that it won't groom you back, and then to never groom that bird again.

We are not merely our biology, and culture and logic may bring us to change our behavior, but there's good reason to believe that this strategy of reciprocal altruism forms the biological basis of human morality. However much or little weight you may put on evolutionary psychology or the role of biology in our thoughts and decisions, it is certainly interesting and heartening to see that, far from a fierce social hierarchy organized under an alpha male, the real "law of the jungle" biologically ingrained in us is fundamentally about *mutual aid*.

How much of a role do you think our biology and evolutionary history play in our social order and ideas of justice and morality?

Elements of culture, like language and at least basic elements of sociality and morality, are embedded in our biology. How do you separate what's "nature" from what's "nurture"?

WHY DO DECENT PEOPLE SOMETIMES DO TERRIBLE THINGS?

In 1961, Stanley Milgram (1933–1984) conducted an experiment at Yale University to see how far people would go to obey authority against their own beliefs. Participants were told they would take part in a study on memory, in which they would read a list of words to the subject, ask the subject to remember the proper word pairs, and administer a shock whenever the subject got it wrong. The shocks increased in intensity as more answers were incorrect, and the strongest shocks were indicated to be dangerous or possibly fatal. The "subject" was an actor, although the participants did not know that. He screamed when the participants thought they were shocking him, and as the "shocks" became more intense, he complained of a heart condition and cried out to be let go and for the experiment to end. The participants were uncomfortable continuing, but were told that the experiment required them to go on. In Milgram's initial experiment and in later recreations of the experiment, almost two-thirds of participants continued to the maximum shock.

Milgram designed the experiment to understand better how the Holocaust could have happened. Is it really possible that so many horrors could have been perpetrated by people who, for the most part, were ordinary, seemingly decent people? The answer seems to be yes. The tendency to obey authority is so strong that many people can be induced with relatively little incentive to do things they believe are wrong.

David Luban, Alan Strudler, and David Wasserman, researchers at the Institute for Philosophy and Public Policy, extended this to the realm of business to see how decent people take part in corporate activities that injure, defraud, and kill. They suggested that we think about getting involved with bureaucracies the same way we think about drinking: Go in with the awareness that your judgment will be impaired once you're in the middle of things, and try to remain aware that you're not fully in control of your own behavior.

When have you done something you believed was wrong because you were "just doing your job"? What would it have cost you to have done the right thing instead?

When have you stood up against procedure, authority, or orders from a superior in order to do what you believed was right? What was the deciding moment for you?

What strategies can you think of that would help you do the right thing in the future, and resist excusing yourself from doing something wrong by saying "Well, I just work here..."?

WHY DO WE NEED FEMINISM?

In what is usually called the "first wave" of feminism, women focused on gaining rights previously given to men alone: for example, rights to vote, inherit property, and hold public office. In the second wave, starting in earnest in the 1960s, women struggled against inequalities that had more to do with social exclusions rather than actual laws limiting the rights of women. The legal right to have a career and live a public life either instead of or in addition to traditional roles means little so long as women are disrespected and so long as the public continues to believe that a woman's place is in the home.

The French philosopher Simone de Beauvoir's (1908–1986) 1949 book *The Second Sex*, a thorough investigation of the meaning of women's experiences and history, played an influential role in the development of feminism. From the title itself we immediately get a sense of the basic view she advanced: Woman has been defined as secondary; "man" is a generic person, and woman is "Other." The Other is defined by opposition to a standard or norm as a kind of exception or deviation. In biology and medicine, as well as in views of history, and perhaps most of all in psychoanalytic theory, women have been defined as altered, incomplete, or mutilated men. At most, women are viewed as "separate but equal," allowing the illusion of parity while men are still viewed as the *real* members of "mankind," as the word itself indicates.

The story of how male and female roles emerged, and how women became the second of the two sexes, is long and complicated, and the solution of granting equal legal recognition is a surface-level fix compared to this cultural history. We must also think through the Otherness of woman.

Picture someone in a position of power and authority—a president, prime minister, CEO, or doctor. In what ways do you think her gender affects how she is viewed and the level of respect given to her by those she directs?

You may not have pictured her as a woman until the second sentence of the previous question, even though the terms used in the first sentence were gender-neutral and apply equally well to men and women. What differences in the lives of women does it make that we assume that those in positions of power and authority are men?

We tend to talk about men as generic people: "he," "man," "mankind." For the next few days, whenever you talk about a generic person or anyone whose gender isn't known, try saying "she" instead of "he" or "they." Then write down here what you learned from the experiment.

ARE TRADITIONAL GENDER ROLES "NATURAL"?

A controversy within feminism concerns how to regard women who choose to adopt traditionally female roles. A truly liberated woman should be free to choose what she wants, but how can we tell whether we are honestly choosing to place family over career, or merely giving in to internalized oppressive prejudices?

Cultural feminism takes a different view of the issue. The central idea is that there really is an essential difference between men and women. Equality shouldn't be about women's ability to do men's work and be considered equal; instead it should be about changing our social values so that women's work and women's virtues are valued as highly as are men's work and men's virtues. In this view, in a male-dominated culture, the values and reward systems of our society have been set up to privilege men, so "women's liberation" in the absence of a change in our values and reward systems just means that women are free to act like men. What if, instead, we changed our society so that raising children, or professions of service and care, were viewed as activities as important and valuable as the stereotypically male pursuits of business and politics—or, at least, changed political and business environments so that they were compatible with and rewarded feminine virtues like collaboration and support rather than masculine virtues of individualistic competition?

An interesting variation of this was brought up by psychiatrist Peter Kramer in his 1993 book *Listening to Prozac*. He asked whether the prevalence of depression among women might be an indication not that many women are mentally ill, but that feminine attributes have been defined as illness. He looked to Victorian feminine ideals—emotional, pensive, moody—and pointed out that today we'd call these symptoms rather than virtues. What if women are being medicated in order to make them act like men and "fit in" better in a male-dominated society?

Is it "only natural" that we see more women in service jobs, early childhood education, and nursing, rather than in positions of more power and authority? Is this a problem we as a society ought to fix?

Maybe the problem isn't that women take on secondary roles, but that we wrongly think of women's roles as secondary. Nurses do most of the care work in healthcare; why don't we view doctors as consultants who play a secondary role in assisting nurses? Early childhood educators, largely female, are underpaid and disrespected, but play a crucial role in the future of our society. Do women tend to take on supporting roles, even though they're lesser roles, because they're drawn to being helpers rather than leaders, or do we think of supporting roles as lesser because women tend to be the ones taking them?

IS THERE SUCH A THING AS A SOUL?

In his *Meditations on First Philosophy*, French philosopher René Descartes gave an argument that he thought showed that the mind is separate from the body and that it survives death. The body, he pointed out, is "extended" (that is, it exists in space, has length and volume, and so on), but does not think. The mind, on the other hand, does think but is not extended. Descartes thought these characteristics could be easily verified through introspection. Consider a thought—where is it? How many cups of water would it hold if you hollowed it out? Imagine cutting it in half: What is half a thought like? How many would you need to make a coat? The other side of the issue seems clear enough as well. We're made of meat and bone, and only a brief conversation with a steak should be enough to convince you that there's not a lot going on in there.

If the mind is thinking and not extended, and the body is extended and not thinking, then they seem to be entirely distinct and separable. So the mind's survival upon the body's death is at least possible. But, further, can there be something like half a mind? Of course not; the mind doesn't have parts!—and so, Descartes argued, the mind cannot decay, and must therefore be eternal, and if the mind is eternal, surely the soul must be as well!

The argument makes some questionable assumptions, of course. Just because things appear to us to be a certain way doesn't make it so. It's true today, as it was then, that we don't entirely understand the connection between the brain as physical matter and the mind as we experience it "from the inside," but we have plenty of evidence that they are different experiences of the same thing. And today we're more likely to think that thoughts are "emergent phenomena"—not really *things* at all, but something more like processes that we call things for convenience.

Do you believe that there is a soul that survives death? What's the basis for your belief?

We know from brain injuries and from electric stimulation of the brain that changes in the brain produce specific and knowable (if complicated) changes in the mind. If you think there is a soul, how does it correspond to the mind? Do changes in the brain affect the soul? Do changes in the mind affect the soul?

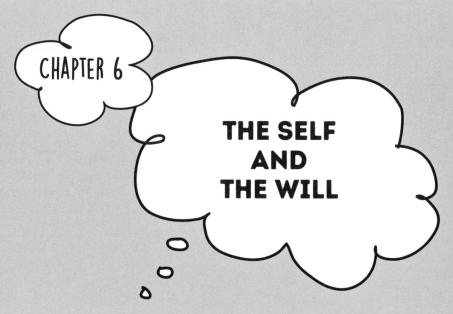

CHAPTER 6

THE SELF AND THE WILL

In this chapter we turn to an assortment of different questions of the will and of the self—questions of choice, of responsibility, and of what sort of thing there is within us that can make choices or can even "have" experiences in the first place. Looking at the mind naturally brings up questions of the mind's relation to the brain and to human evolution; it also brings up questions of the mind's relation to the soul and our possible fate after death.

As in previous chapters, the questions here may require you to play along with some assumptions. By turns, I'll ask you to adopt, at least temporarily, assumptions of the evolutionary origin of the species, Judeo-Christian assumptions about God and sin, and assumptions of reincarnation from Buddhist and Hindu religions.

WHY DO WE HAVE MINDS?

William James (1842–1910), an American Pragmatist philosopher and psychologist, considered *epiphenomenalism*—the idea that mental events, like thoughts, experiences, and intentions, are just aftereffects that play no actual role in determining what we do. If this is true, all our decisions are made through unconscious processes, and conscious experience just hangs around making up explanations after the fact. The epiphenomenalist believes that mental experiences are like the smoke rising from a train: They are only a by-product that is produced along the way. All the real work happens down below in the engine room.

There's something to be said for this view. Sometimes, when we are startled—as, for example, when hearing a sudden noise while walking through the woods at night—we react first and only feel afraid once we have already begun to run away. In the end, though, James thought that evolutionary biology indicates that epiphenomenalism must be wrong. If you go back far enough in evolutionary history, there must have been a time when minds and mental experiences did not exist. So consciousness and thought evolved at some point, and if consciousness plays no role in determining our actions, why would these things have come into being? How could they be evolutionarily adaptive unless they are part of a feedback loop? The process goes like this: Our consciousness is stimulated by the environment and, in turn, plays a role in determining our actions in that environment.

And yet couldn't it be that the feedback loop is adaptive and effective, but our consciousness of it is still just an aftereffect? But if this is the case, then why wouldn't we simply have brains, but not *minds*?

Do you believe we have free will? Why?

What would your experience be like if we don't have free will? Would you be able to tell?

DO WE ALWAYS HAVE FREE WILL?

The French existentialist Jean-Paul Sartre thought not only that we have free will, but that our choice is *always* undetermined. One place he thinks we can see this is in the experience of vertigo.

Sartre says that the experience of vertigo is not a fear of falling. If you pay attention to what it actually feels like next time you're up high near an edge, you'll see it's a kind of excited agitation, not fear. Also, we experience vertigo even when there's no realistic risk, like when we are on good footing and there is a solid railing. He says vertigo is actually a feeling caused by the awareness that at the next moment we could choose to throw ourselves over the edge. It's not that we *want* to, even secretly or subconsciously, but that, even though every fiber of our being shouts "No!" we are still aware that in the very next moment we could suddenly decide otherwise and that our current resolve does nothing to diminish our freedom in the next moment.

Along the same lines, he asks us to consider a gambler (although any kind of addict works equally well). The gambler may choose with full resolve not to gamble, but as soon as the question comes up again—perhaps friends are getting together for cards, or there's merely an idle hour in the day and a casino nearby—they have to decide again. Their previous resolve doesn't save them from having to decide again every day and every moment that the question presents itself.

In this way at the very least, we always experience ourselves as possessed of a radical freedom: not only able, but *condemned* to choose.

Most people believe we have a free will, but our choices are conditioned by circumstances, history, mood, and a variety of other factors. It's best not to go grocery shopping while you're hungry, for example. How can you tell when your choice is under some influence or another?

Even when we aren't choosing entirely freely, we feel as if we are—at least while we're making the choice. But aren't there some circumstances in which you aren't just influenced in your decisions, but really aren't responsible for your actions?

If you said yes to the previous question, isn't it still true that you could have chosen otherwise in these "determined" circumstances? Isn't your will always basically free, then?

DOES GOD KNOW WHAT WE ARE GOING TO CHOOSE BEFORE WE CHOOSE IT?

Christians believe that there is an omniscient God, and if God is all-knowing, it seems as if God must know what we are going to do before we do it. But if God knows what we're going to do before we do it, then there must be some knowable fact about what we are going to do, and that fact must exist before we do it. But if there's a fact about what we're going to do before we do it, then how could it be that we have free will, since there's already a fact about what we will have chosen while we are choosing to do it? If there's already a fact about what we will choose, that seems to mean that we can't choose otherwise; therefore, we don't have free will. And if we don't have free will, then we're not responsible for our actions, in which case surely it's wrong to judge us on what we do. Which is to say that God's judgment must be unjust.

Did you get all that? Do you see the problem? It's weird stuff, but it makes sense once you're in the middle of it.

The issue was actually explored brilliantly in "Minority Report," a short story about "precrime" written by Philip K. Dick (1928–1982) in the 1950s. (You may be more familiar with the film *Minority Report*, which is less brilliant, but contains significantly more chase scenes, for what it's worth.) How can there be free will if there's foreknowledge of choices that will be made? And how can punishment for predetermined crimes be justified?

St. Anselm of Canterbury (1033–1109) presented an elegant solution. He claimed that the confusion is created by the false premise that God exists in time. God, he said, exists outside of time itself, and so He sees all times as if they were present at once. The progress of time moves forward and the future is always open, and yet God can see the future even though (from our perspective, in time) the future doesn't even exist and really is entirely undetermined.

Thinking about things from a monotheistic perspective for now, if you have free will, does God know what you will choose?

If God doesn't know what you'll choose, why not, if God is omniscient and omnipotent? If God does know what you'll choose, why does He let you choose to do bad things?

If God lets you do bad things when He could have stopped you, is it fair to punish you for doing what He could have stopped? Or, if it's fair to punish you for your intention alone, why not stop you from doing something and just punish you for what you would have done?

ARE OTHER PEOPLE REAL?

Given that we can put together a purely physical and causal account of how bodies and nervous systems result in action, it seems like the only reason we know for sure about conscious experiences is that we have them. But what if not everybody does? Is it possible that at least some other humans are just very complicated biological mechanisms without a will or inner experiences?

As far as I know, Descartes was the first to bring up this kind of question, and it makes sense that it would have arisen in Europe in the seventeenth century. At that time, automata, or self-moving machines, were a popular amusement among the wealthy. For example, a nude statue in a hedge maze might be "automated" so that when someone stepped on a hidden switch as they came around the corner, the statue would turn to cover itself in modesty. Descartes asked his reader to imagine looking outside a window: We say that we see people going by, when in fact the senses only tell us that we see umbrellas and coats, which could as easily be a series of dressed-up automata passing by. Reason, not our senses, tells us that they are people.

Now, Descartes's point was just about whether we know what we know based on reason or on the senses. The more radical question is how we can be sure that there's an "inside" inside of other people at all. The most popular answer has been that we know this by analogy. We act a certain way, and mental experiences accompany those actions, so it stands to reason that others have similar mental experiences when they act in similar ways.

We can supplement this with some biological considerations. We know that colors, for example, correspond to different wavelengths of light and that our eyes and brains are constituted in definable and functionally equivalent ways, and this supports the idea that the experience of light with a wavelength around 700 nanometers should be not only consistently *called* red, but also consistently *experienced* as red.

The uncertainty of this, though, is still troubling. The what-it's-like, or *qualia*, of a physical experience seems unrelated to the physical basis. There's no "redness" in the wavelength, or in the eye, or in the synapses of the brain. Similarly, although there may be physical phenomena in the brain associated with the experience of pain, there's nothing *painlike* to be found there—and consciousness itself isn't something we can point to either.

Is it possible that what you call "red" is experienced by others as what you call "green"? Is there any way you could tell?

Is it possible that what you experience as pain is experienced by others as soothing, and they just happen to enjoy pain and dislike being soothed? Is there any way you could tell?

Is it possible that some other people aren't conscious and don't have thoughts but are just very complicated biological mechanisms without a will or inner experiences? Is there any way you could tell?

ARE YOU THE SAME YOU AS YESTERDAY?

If it's troubling to think that other people might not have consciousness, that seems to indicate that we think the "self" is in consciousness rather than in just the brain or body. But what happens when we lose consciousness? How do we know when we wake up in the morning that we're the same person that we remember from yesterday? Is it possible that every "consciousness" is a different person, and that we die when we go to sleep, and the person who wakes up the next day with our memories is someone else?

The English philosopher John Locke would say, "Sure, why not?" In his view, we have no way of knowing that each of us is a single self, or that we are the same selves that we were. The only clue we have about whether the self is constant over time is continuity of consciousness, and past the present moment that boils down to memory. But Locke didn't want to conclude that the self is temporary or unstable, but instead that what we mean by "the self" is just this continuity of consciousness. So if

you remember being yesterday-you, then it doesn't really make sense to even ask whether yesterday-you might have died, to be replaced by today-you (or, in other words, *you*-you). What you mean by saying that that was you yesterday *is nothing else* but that yesterday-you's experiences belong to you as yours.

Locke gave a few more examples to show that it is *consciousness* that makes us who we are, not some underlying substance. If you lose a hand, there is no question that you continue to be the same person. If, on the other hand (so to speak), consciousness were located in our little fingers, we would say that *the finger* remains the person even if it's severed from the rest of the body. Locke also considered the soul of a prince suddenly entering the body of a cobbler, which he imagined basically like a two-way brain transplant. If consciousness and memory are continuous from the old bodies to the new ones, surely we'd say that the people switched *bodies*, not that they switched brains.

Imagine it's true that you were a different person yesterday, and you die every night and someone else wakes up in your (former) body the next day with your memories. Is that distressing? Why?

Is it possible that there are two of you right now, but you're unaware of each other, and you simply share the same memories as if you had each experienced them?

Is it possible that, five minutes ago, you switched bodies and memories with someone else? If you're out in public, look to your right. Could you have been that person just a few minutes ago?

IS THE SELF A THING?

For Scottish philosopher David Hume (1711–1776), questions about the yesterday-you and today-you would have been a load of crap. To even think that they make sense, you have to make a big metaphysical assumption: that there is some kind of "self" that "has" experiences and hangs around behind the scenes through your whole life. But what basis is there for such a belief? We don't have any experience of a "self" at all. Sure, everything we experience is experienced as *our* experience, but we don't have any experience of being a thing that *has* those experiences—we only experience the experiences. "The mind," Hume wrote, "is a kind of theatre, where several perceptions successively make their appearance." But even this analogy is flawed, because it implies at least a constant *stage* upon which these experiences appear. Hume added that "the comparison of the theatre must not mislead us. They are the successive perceptions only, that constitute the mind; nor have we the most distant notion of the place, where these scenes are represented, or of the materials, of which it is compos'd."

Hume had no patience for things we would like to believe when there's no evidence to support them, and this is abundantly clear in this case. What else could we believe more strongly than that we exist as subjects, as things which our experiences *happen to*? And yet our experience is entirely and precisely devoid of any experience of the self: When we try to imagine the self that undergoes an experience, we find that it has no qualities or attributes apart from the experience it is undergoing. Worse yet, when we try to contemplate the "self" having the experience, we find that the self has already retreated! Try it—you'll find that you are no longer the you having the experience. Instead you've become the you that is experiencing contemplating the "you" that had the experience. And now that you're thinking about *that*, you're another step removed (and now, another [and now, another (and so on)]).

In the previous entry we were considering whether the yesterday-you is the same you as the today-you. What does that even mean? What is the "you" that has your experiences, and have you had any experiences of it?

What if "self" is just a word we use to indicate which experiences have the same history, and each *moment* of consciousness is connected only by memory to previous moments? Is that frightening or disorienting?

Why do we feel a pull toward the idea of a constant "self" that "has" experiences and is the same thing through our lives?

DOES THE WILL TO LIVE TRAP US?

In the previous entries there's a good chance that you connected our anxiety about having a constant "self" to our fear of death. If the "self" of consciousness isn't constant through our own lives, it seems like there's little hope that it will survive death. This can also give us some insight on why we care about the idea that we might survive death.

In the nineteenth century, philosophical works from Asia were becoming available to Europeans, and German philosopher Arthur Schopenhauer developed a theory of the self strongly influenced by Buddhism and by the Hindu Vedas. He thought that just as we ourselves appear in two aspects—to the senses and to science we appear as a thing, but in our inner experience we experience ourselves as thought and will—so too is everything in reality both matter and will. Will is the "inner truth" and reality of the world. The will, then, is not destroyed by death. The body becomes soil, and then plants, and then animals, and then soil again, as the will is expressed as the nutrients in the soil, then as the growth of the plants, and then as the movement and hungers of the animals. Individuality dies, but the will, as the animating principle of the world, is indestructible.

Schopenhauer presented this in a dialogue, where he imagined the anguished reply, "*I* want to exist! That is what I care about, and not an existence which has to be reasoned out first in order to show that it is mine." This, Schopenhauer thinks, is ridiculous. The "I" of the will, the "subject" that undergoes experiences and wills to live, is the *least* distinctive and individual thing about us! The drive to preserve the self traps us in an unending cycle of desire, and life becomes nothing but the constant cycle from the pain of desire to the boredom of satisfaction. We should seek instead, not that the "I" should survive death, but that the "I" should be destroyed within life in a Buddhistic "negation of the will." Even death does not quiet the will. Only ceasing the cycle of desire by destroying the self can free us from the will and from suffering.

Do you believe in any kind of reincarnation or transmigration of souls? If so, what kind, and why?

Most people don't have memories of past lives, so it seems that if any kind of transmigration occurs, it usually includes memory loss. But if memories are lost, what is it, exactly, that is transferred?

Assume for the moment that after your death you will become someone else but have no memory of having been who you are today. Why would you care? Would that be any different *to you* than if you were entirely annihilated rather than reborn?

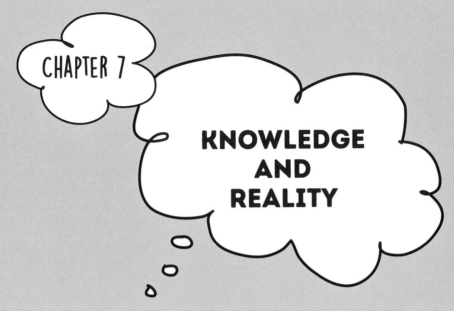

CHAPTER 7

KNOWLEDGE AND REALITY

There are a wealth of different philosophical issues having to do with what's real and how (and whether) we can know about it. Many of these questions appear in the other chapters—questions of knowledge and reality are at the base of most of the questions in this book—but this chapter will look at questions having to do specifically with what knowledge is, and how it connects us or fails to connect us with reality outside of the mind.

If you have some philosophical training, you may be disappointed that we're passing over some major issues. Some topics within questions of knowledge and reality, though very important within academic philosophy today, are too technical and deeply embedded with the history and context of scholarly argumentation to present well in a short, concise form. I've left out some worthy topics, but this selection will give you a good sense of how philosophers talk about these issues, and should provide a good basis for some interesting conversations!

WHAT IS ALL THIS STUFF?

Have you ever noticed how if you keep saying the same word over and over again, it starts to seem really weird? "Is that how that word is spelled?" "What does that word mean, exactly?" This is what's called *semantic saturation*, and the same thing happens when you think about an idea for long enough. "Stuff" is a weird word, but it's not nearly as weird as stuff itself is, when you think about it long enough.

The ancient Greek philosopher Thales (c. 624–c. 546 B.C.E.) is often called the first philosopher in the European tradition, and his main idea was that everything is made out of water. Now you're probably thinking, *lolwut?* Actually, it's not nearly as weird as it sounds. Things undergo change, so there must be some *underlying stuff* that things are made from that is the stuff that undergoes the change. Things don't just appear and disappear. As to what that underlying stuff is, water is actually a pretty good candidate. We can see how water changes into ice or into steam. Water is taken up by plants and becomes their leaves and fruit, and it replenishes our bodies as well. It's stuff that a lot of things are made of.

Other philosophers around the same time had different theories. Anaximander (c. 610–c. 546 B.C.E.) said the underlying stuff was undefined, but became different things through heat, cold, moisture, and dryness. Pythagoras (c. 570–c. 495 B.C.E.) thought the basis of things was mathematical. Heraclitus (c. 535–c. 475 B.C.E.) said everything was fire, but he might have meant that metaphorically—fire is a process, not stuff, and he said that the only constant unchanging thing in the world was change itself. Parmenides (c. 515–c. 450 B.C.E.) went the other direction and said change is an illusion and there is only a single unchanging thing. Democritus (c. 460–c. 370 B.C.E.) even claimed that all the things were really made of tiny indivisible things (the Greek word is *atom*) that combine in different forms to make things. So some of these ideas might sound familiar.

There's a bunch of stuff everywhere, right? What's it made of? And what is that stuff made of? Is there some basic stuff that all other stuff is made of? If so, what's it made of?

Some things sometimes become other things—like how ice melts. When things become other things, is it still the same stuff? If it is, then why isn't it the same anymore? If it isn't, then what happened—did some stuff get added or taken away from the other stuff?

All this stuff got here from somewhere—presumably from other stuff, because stuff doesn't just show up; stuff is made out of stuff. How did all this different stuff end up being so different? Is all this stuff really different stuff? Mustn't it be that all this different stuff is really the same, because it's all made out of the same stuff?

ARE LAWS OF NATURE CONSISTENT?

When we say something is a "law of nature," it seems like we mean that it's permanent, unchanging, and constant. But Scottish philosopher David Hume pointed out that experimental scientific observation doesn't provide the right kind of evidence to let us say anything about whether any patterns, no matter how constant, are *necessary* and will *definitely* stay the same.

Inductive reasoning, where we use particular instances to demonstrate a general rule, seemed to him to be suspicious in a very basic way. How many cases are enough to establish that things will *always* and *necessarily* work a certain way? Assume some number of cases, n, is enough. What did the nth case have that the n-1 case didn't? Wouldn't we need an infinite number of cases to show that it will *always* and *necessarily* work out that way?

Worse yet, the very idea of using different cases (for example, dropping a series of different objects) to establish a "law" (e.g., gravity) is dependent on the idea

that nature is consistent—that the future will be like the past. If the future isn't like the past, then past evidence doesn't have any predictive value at all. But what evidence do we have that the future will be like the past? The only evidence is that *in the past* the future has always been like the past, so it seems like *in the future* the future will also be like the past. But it would obviously be bad reasoning to assume the consistency of nature in order to provide evidence for the consistency of nature.

And we can't observe or reason out these connections between events directly either. There's nothing "drowninglike" about water—the only way to find out that it can't be breathed is the hard way. Same thing with the coldness of ice, or the saltiness of salt, or the "fallingness" of things heavier than air. If these causal structures had a logical basis, then we could know that they will always and necessarily be that way, but because we only find out these connections through experience, we can only make claims about them through inductive reasoning. Which, according to the arguments we just went through, seems arbitrary and unjustified. So Hume thought that the way the universe works isn't something we can know for certain, and that every scientific theory, in the end, will always be just a theory.

How does gravity work? Try to really explain it in ordinary, nontechnical language.

We all know *that* gravity works, at least. Could mass start to repel itself instead of attracting itself, as of tomorrow? Is there anything any less likely about repelling than attracting, or anything about mass that makes it make more sense somehow that it would attract other mass rather than repel it?

Why couldn't the laws of nature change suddenly? Is there a law of nature that the laws of nature can't change? Why can't that law change?

IS EVERYTHING YOU BELIEVE ABOUT THE WORLD WRONG?

Immanuel Kant, inspired by the deeply troubling problems about knowledge brought up by David Hume, wrote his monumental *Critique of Pure Reason*, in which he tried to show what kinds of things are within the realm of human knowledge, and what kinds of things aren't. To get at this, he first identified the structures that allow us to think and perceive things at all, including forms of the senses (space and time) and categories of the understanding (like "substance" and "cause and effect"). These structures make experience *possible*, so there is literally no possible way we can know if they're true. For example, if we saw something that existed but didn't exist in space, we'd either experience it as if it did exist in space or we wouldn't experience it at all, because the ideas of "seeing" and "thing" only make sense at all *in the form of space*. So if "space" wasn't real, there's no way we could ever find that out.

And consider this: How did you learn that space and time are empty and infinite, that the first

has three dimensions and the second has only one? There's no way you could have learned that from experience, since you've never had an experience of *just* space, or of empty time. These are structures that make experience possible, not things outside of the mind.

So, we can't show that these "forms of perception" are real because if they were false, we'd never know. The same is true for concepts like substance and causality. We have no direct experience of them as things. In fact, any experiences of things require that we assume there are substances; otherwise, we can't organize different impressions like color, smell, and texture into an experience of a thing. We have to assume causality as well, since even the idea of "observing" or "evidence" is going to assume a cause-and-effect relationship between some thing and our observation. These are all conditions for the possibility of experience, and that means that experience will always happen on the assumption that these conditions are real, so no experience will ever prove or disprove them.

But could they still happen to be true, even if we can't prove it? Yes, for sure! Unless, of course, someone—maybe *Immanuel Kant*—asked some uncomfortable questions that demonstrated they can't possibly be true because they lead to logical contradictions...

Imagine anything. Maybe a stick. Imagine cutting it in half. Now again. Now again. And so on. Can you keep dividing it in half infinitely? If so, what would you have left at the end of the infinity of dividing? If what you have left is something, then the original stick was infinite, since an infinite amount of anything is infinite. But if what you have left in the end is nothing, then there was no stick, since an infinite amount of nothing is nothing. Is there something wrong with the stick, or something wrong with this reasoning?

Let's back up and assume that at some point you can't divide the thing in half anymore. That indivisible thing: Does it have length? If it does, then you can divide it in half, and you haven't yet reached the point when you can't divide it in half anymore. But if it doesn't have length, then it can't be a thing! So, there's no stick, right?

Okay, how about this: Does the universe have a beginning? If so, something must have started it, so you're not at the beginning yet. But then what started the starting? And what started that? On the other hand, if it doesn't have a beginning, how can it exist? Something can't be happening if it never started, right? Right?

HOW IS IT POSSIBLE THAT YOU KNOW ANYTHING?

Here's a problem philosophers have been kicking around for a couple millennia, sometimes called "Agrippa's Trilemma":

- **Premise 1:** You know something.
- **Premise 2:** Knowledge requires justification.
- **Premise 3:** Nothing can be its own justification.
- **Conclusion:** Knowledge requires an infinite series of justifications.

Unless we think it makes sense you are (somehow) currently at the end of an infinity of justifications, we're going to have to drop one of our premises. We could deny the first premise and say that knowledge is impossible, or we could deny the second premise by claiming that some forms of knowledge don't require reasons at all, or we could deny the third premise and say that some forms of knowledge can be evidence for themselves.

Philosophers have pursued all three options. The first is the position of the skeptic. The second is the position of "foundationalism," which claims that some things can be "the end of the line" in reason-giving. Usually, the foundations given are sense data, but Descartes tried the foundation of self-knowledge. "I exist" doesn't need a justification, in his view, because as soon as we doubt it, we find that we are there, doing the doubting! But getting from "I think, therefore I am" to any knowledge about anything else is, well, hard to argue convincingly. The third option is "coherentism," which is the view that there are no foundational beliefs, and no ends to the process of giving reasons, but that it's okay for reason-giving to be circular. In this view, the internal coherence and consistency of a big set of beliefs gives all of them a collective justification. So you might not be able to prove that you're not asleep and dreaming right now, but the coherence of the different clues, cues, and observations that support that idea gives you reason enough to say you know you're awake.

Which seems like the right path to you?

Assume for a moment that you know something. Anything at all. If you know it to be true, there must be some reason why. But you have to know that reason, too, so there must be a reason you know that reason to be true. And so on. Can't we just keep asking "But why?" over and over again?

Is it possible that there are some things that we know, but which we don't need to give reasons for? Some things that are self-justifying?

If there aren't some self-justifying "foundational" things that we know, can we really know anything? Is there an "end of the line" in explaining why you know what you know?

CAN YOU BELIEVE WHATEVER YOU WANT?

A shipowner hasn't kept up with regular maintenance, but he decides to think positive and manifest his desire that his ship is still okay. So, when he rents the ship and it sinks and everybody aboard drowns, he is as shocked and saddened as anyone and has an untroubled conscience, since he honestly and earnestly believed that the ship was safe. What exactly has he done wrong?

This case comes from English philosopher W.K. Clifford (1845–1879), who used it as the starting point of his famous essay "The Ethics of Belief." Clifford argued that it is always wrong to hold beliefs in the absence of sufficient evidence of their truth, and that it is similarly always wrong to ignore evidence that goes against our beliefs. It's not just a personal choice to believe whatever makes us feel good or righteous or comfortable, because our beliefs affect others as soon as we act on them! So Clifford said we have a responsibility to those around us to form our beliefs in a responsible manner and to make sure they're justified by testing our beliefs whenever we have reason to.

This process—epistemic responsibility—is pretty difficult. Like the shipowner, we are too easily seduced by self-interest into disregarding "inconvenient truths." What's more, we often fail to notice evidence contrary to our beliefs because of confirmation bias, which makes us focus instead on the evidence that fits with what we already believe.

Here's an example that shows how easily our attention brings us to bad beliefs. Imagine you've got one hundred employees and some of them are stealing from you. You give all your employees a lie-detector test that's 80 percent accurate, and the test identifies twenty-six of the employees as lying about not stealing. Consider each person identified by the test as a thief. For each person, how likely is it that they are actually stealing from you? Stop reading here, think about it for a minute, and settle on an answer.

Okay, you're back. Most people would say there's an 80 percent chance. That's because we focus on catching the thieves, and don't pay enough attention to the effect that the test has on the innocent. The answer is actually only 30.8 percent! Do you see why?

If the test is 80 percent accurate, you'll correctly identify 80 percent of the thieves. But the test is also wrong 20 percent of the time, so it'll incorrectly identify 20 percent of the innocent people. And if it identified twenty-six people as thieves, that means you've actually only got ten thieves, and your pool of twenty-six includes eight of them (80 percent of the ten guilty employees) and another eighteen innocents (20 percent of the ninety innocent employees). And that means only 30.8 percent, eight out of twenty-six, of your pool of identified people are actually guilty.

This is just one example of how quickly things like focus, self-interest, and confirmation bias can make epistemic responsibility difficult. And this is in the realm of things we can see and test! In religious and moral beliefs, where solid evidence can't be presented, the problem of responsibility in acting on your beliefs seems more difficult.

Do you believe that some lifestyles are more moral or righteous than others? Can you point to evidence for that belief? Have you tested your belief by trying to falsify it? Would it be responsible for you to act on your belief?

One time when my son was six, he came to tell me that he needed paper towels, since his sister had spilled some mouthwash as they were getting ready for bed. As I got the paper towels I asked him whether it was a big spill or a little spill. "I don't know," he said. "I haven't seen most spills."

How much epistemic responsibility is too much? How do you know where to draw the line?

WHAT'S WITH ALL THIS BULLSHIT?

Harry Frankfurt (1929–), a contemporary American philosopher, explored the phenomenon of bullshit in an essay appropriately titled "On Bullshit," which has since been published as a stand-alone book. He's obviously quite right to identify bullshit as a significant aspect of our society, worthy of careful consideration, although there are perhaps some obvious reasons why other philosophers hadn't published a whole lot on the topic.

In Frankfurt's analysis, bullshit is characterized by a lack of concern for the truth. In lies, there is a matter of fact that the liar is concerned with, even if that concern is to *hide* it. The bullshitter, on the other hand, isn't concerned with covering up some matter of fact, but instead wants to cover up the truth about his own *intention* in speaking. The bullshitter might even say things that are true! Frankfurt considers a politician bullshitting through a Fourth of July speech. They might say a lot of nice things about liberty and founding principles and whatever, some of which may be true or even insightful, but the speaker's concern is not with history or political philosophy—the speaker's concern is that they want the audience to see them as someone who cares about all that stuff. To give an example from advertising, consider the claims "100 Percent Natural" and "Contains a clinically tested ingredient." Both may be true, but that doesn't mean they aren't bullshit. They're not there to inform you, or to lie to you. They're there to make you buy things.

We professors see a lot of bullshitting in student writing. Student bullshitting consists largely of vague claims that could well be true, but which are directed at *taking up space* and *sounding on topic* rather than actually providing information or analysis. Information and analysis, after all, can be identified as wrong, which will lose points on the assignment. Student bullshitting seeks to finish out the assignment while providing as little to grasp onto as possible…not unlike much political rhetoric.

If that sounds familiar, don't feel bad. It's a rational response for students to bullshit assignments when they think the only important thing about the material is being able to look like you know it. The real problem isn't the student, or the advertiser, or the politician. The real problem is an educational system that focuses on assessment rather than learning, a market driven by fears and desires rather than facts and needs, and a political environment focused on perception rather than policy.

Harry Frankfurt claims that "One of the most salient features of our culture is that there is so much bullshit. Everyone knows this." Is bullshitting uniquely connected to contemporary American culture? How did it come to be so central to our society?

Besides politics and advertising, where else do you see a lot of bullshitting? When was the last time you had to bullshit something, maybe for your job?

Sometimes we "cut the bullshit" or tell someone "I'm not going to bullshit you." Can you remember a time when you decided to keep it real? Can you remember a time when you wish you had bullshitted instead of keeping it real?

CHAPTER 8

SCIENCE

There's a great deal at stake for us in questions of the meaning, structure, and importance of science, and a great many of these questions are much thornier and troubling than most of us appreciate. Science is something of a given for us today—we believe in the certainty of its claims, and in the consistent forward progress of scientific knowledge—but when pressed on how science works or the concept of science itself, what makes science scientific, it slips easily through our fingers.

This chapter will start with three entries on what science is, looking at its relationship to religion and to mathematics, and how working out those relationships helped to establish how we understand science today as an experimental and empirical learning process that makes progress but will never be finished. The entries after that will look at different views on how science makes progress and moves from one theory to another better theory, considering the role of confirmation, falsification, and prediction. After that, we'll look at whether scientific theories are true, or are aiming to be true, or if they're just supposed to be useful. The final entry will look at where the successes of science have gotten us, and what it will take for us to survive our own newfound abilities.

ARE SCIENCE AND RELIGION ALWAYS AT ODDS?

"Science" is a relatively recent development of what used to be known as "natural philosophy," and philosophers of nature have run into resistance from religious perspectives from the very beginning. Socrates was accused of believing the sun was just a burning rock rather than the chariot of the god Apollo, although he claimed that he thought no such thing, and he was sentenced to death for impiety.

We already discussed some of these early Greek *physiologoi*—philosophers of nature—at the beginning of the previous chapter, like Thales, who thought that everything was water, or Democritus, who thought things were made out of "atoms." Anaxagoras (c. 500–c. 428 B.C.E.) was another one of these physiologoi, and he's the one who actually did claim that the sun was burning iron. He also worked on explanations of eclipses and the planets and came up with the idea that the moon shone by reflecting the light of the sun. Like Socrates, he was charged with impiety. For a society that we view today as sophisticated

and philosophical, Athens was surprisingly prone to sentencing philosophers to death or exile for impiety.

Athenian government was based in religion—Athens's legitimacy was said to come from the goddess Athena—and Greek religion was much more concerned with explaining nature than religious views today, which tend to view God as a creator and planner rather than an active force in the day-to-day workings of the world. Religion has mostly retreated from making claims about planets, wind, crops, and natural history, but in ancient Greece the idea that we should try to figure out these things through reason and observation, rather than accepting the traditional stories, was still very dangerous. After all, if we start coming up with theories of nature, well, the next step might be trying to run the state based on reason and evidence rather than the traditional grounding of civil authority in the will of the gods.

What seem to you to be the most obvious possible conflicts between scientific and religious views?

Are there ways of making these religious and scientific views compatible?

What kinds of religious views can't be made compatible with views based in science?

DOES SCIENCE DEPEND MORE ON MATH OR ON OBSERVATION?

Even though the most famous parts of Descartes's *Meditations on First Philosophy* are his radical, solipsistic doubt (How do I know I'm not asleep? Is an evil demon deceiving me by making me think that the world and other people exist?) and the cogito (I think, therefore I am), which helped him overcome that doubt, his actual *point* in the *Meditations* was to establish a scientific method that would allow "natural philosophy" to proceed with something like the same kind of certainty as mathematics, and to convince the Church not to oppose such a scientific method.

Descartes thought that the problem was that science had depended too much on the senses and not enough on reason. Heliocentrism was one of the controversies of the day, and Descartes, like Galileo, believed that the earth revolved around the sun, rather than the other way around. The problem was that in commonsense observations, the earth below us certainly seemed to be stable and not hurtling through space, and the sun obviously moved in the sky. Furthermore, on the Church's reading of the Bible, it said clearly that the earth was fixed. The main factor in favor of heliocentrism was that it made for a more elegant mathematical model of the movement of the planets.

In the *Meditations*, Descartes tried to show that the senses weren't trustworthy, and that we needed a form of science based in reason and mathematics *first*, and observations only secondarily. Along the way, he also tried to provide proofs of God's existence and goodness as well as proof of an immortal human soul—after all, if his argument could prove these elements of faith *and* establish a mathematically based science, then the Church would be able to see that science in general and heliocentrism in particular were compatible with faith.

What role does mathematics play in science? Is mathematics just used to make sense of observations? Or does mathematics play a more active role in determining what those observations mean or even what sorts of things to make observations about?

What's at stake in this issue—that is, what difference does it make whether mathematics plays a leading or a supporting role in scientific inquiry?

WHY IS MATH MORE CERTAIN THAN SCIENCE?

Descartes thought that a mathematically based science could achieve something like the same kind of certainty as mathematics. Why didn't this work out?

Immanuel Kant gave a very convincing explanation in his *Critique of Pure Reason*, published in 1781. He argued that space and time aren't real things in the world outside of us, but are just the forms in which we perceive things—necessary conditions for the possibility of human experience. So any experience we will ever have will take place in space and time because those are the structures we use to experience things.

Geometry, Kant said, is nothing but an exploration of space. Space comes with a set of rules already in place, and when we discover the relationships already there in the concept of space, we are discovering things that will always be true of everything we'll ever experience in the world, because we'll always experience it in space. Furthermore, because space is part of our internal workings, so to speak, it never changes, unlike things in the world, so proving something once is enough to make it true for all

experiences by all humans for all time!

Arithmetic, similarly, is an exploration of time. When we add, we are saying in effect, "First this, and then that, and that makes two events." Everything else follows from there. So it's not accidental that we think of a "number line" going from infinite negative numbers to infinite positive numbers, with a zero in the middle, just as we think of time as taking place in one dimension, stretching infinitely into the past in one direction and into the future in the other, with the present right in the middle.

And this is why we can't put together a scientific method that will provide knowledge as certain and permanent and universal as mathematics! Science is about the world beyond our perception as we can access it through experimental observation, so it will always have only theories and never certain knowledge. Mathematics can have certain, universal, and permanent knowledge, but only because it's about our forms of perception and understanding and *not* about the world itself.

Kant's view on why and how mathematics works can be hard to accept. Try to propose a different explanation for how people can come up with a bunch of facts about triangles by just thinking about them, and then find out that they turn out to be true in the world as well—and true with absolute certainty, and for all time. What are other possible explanations, and are any of them better?

If mathematics isn't based on our own forms of perception, what else could it be based on? We never observe triangles or numbers, but we do *draw* and *measure* and *count*. If you think about these human activities of ordering and making sense of the world as the basis of mathematics, then Kant's claim is that mathematics is the abstract study of how humans order and make sense of things in space and in time. Does that make more sense? What is still difficult or unclear about this view?

WHAT COUNTS AS EVIDENCE FOR SCIENTIFIC THEORIES?

So science can only provide theories, not absolute certainty. But some theories are obviously better than others! What makes one better supported than another?

A good starting place is the idea that observations that fit with the predictions hypothesized by the theory provide evidence in its favor. For example, if your theory is that "all ravens are black," and you go out and look at a bunch of ravens and hey, yep, they're all black, then your reasons for believing the theory just got better, right? Carl Hempel (1905–1997), a German philosopher of science, said, unfortunately, no. And it's not because there are in fact albino ravens. Just ignore that. The problem applies equally well to any empirical claim; "water is liquid at room temperature," for example.

Here's the problem: "All ravens are black" is logically equivalent to the claim that "all non-black things are non-ravens." This implies that, if looking at ravens and finding them to be black provides evidence in favor of the claim "all ravens are black," then you can also provide evidence in favor of "all ravens are black" by looking at the white thing in front of you and making a note that it is a page in this book and not a raven. And this seems to present a serious problem! A view of science that says that we can practice "indoor ornithology" by walking around the house looking at non-black things and observing that they are also non-ravens seems to have gone seriously astray somewhere.

Philosophers have tried to dismiss Hempel's "Raven Paradox" in many different ways, but some philosophers, including Hempel himself, have accepted it. Why?

The silliness of doing "indoor ornithology" this way is actually an excellent clue. If you did look at a red or green or other non-black thing and found out it *was* a raven, it would disconfirm your theory, so *logically speaking* it's not an absurd thing to do. What makes it absurd then? Hempel would say that it's because you have a pretty good idea of whether or not there are ravens in your house.

If we look at a less intuitive claim, like his example "all sodium salts burn yellow," this might be clearer. If you burn an unknown substance and it burns yellow, it's really pretty reasonable to check whether it contains sodium salts, and if it doesn't, to count that as evidence in favor of the claim. The "paradox" only seems paradoxical because we smuggled in assumptions like "the thing I put in the flame doesn't have any sodium salts in it" or "I don't have a bunch of birds lying around the house."

Another possibility is to say the idea that scientific theories are confirmed through observation is just plain doomed. We already saw one argument along that line from Hume, in the previous chapter on knowledge and reality. But if scientific theories aren't supported by confirming observations, how do we know which theories are better than others—and if we don't know which theories are better than others, how have we made progress in scientific knowledge?

There are many more non-black things than there are ravens. Could it be that checking ravens for non-blackness provides better evidence than checking non-black things for ravenness because it subjects the theory to more risk of being proven wrong?

Maybe inductive evidence and the idea of confirming a scientific theory really don't make sense. In this case, the most we could say for a scientific theory is that it hasn't been disproven (yet). Would that be enough to explain how science progresses, and to reflect the strength of scientific knowledge?

HOW DO YOU FIGURE OUT WHICH THEORIES ARE BETTER?

The view that observations that fit with a theory provide *no evidence at all* for believing the theory was defended by another German philosopher of science, Karl Popper (1902–1994). To give you a quick view of why this view might be right, consider the competing theories (a) ice melts at room temperature and (b) hidden liquid-demons transform ice into water unless it is so cold that the demons fall asleep. We can provide a lot of evidence that fits with either theory, but that doesn't mean that they're both good theories.

Popper's *falsificationist* view of scientific progress says that we don't get to better theories through confirmation, but by falsification. In this view, a mountain of evidence that fits with a theory makes not a bit of difference in how certain that theory is. Even if it's the going theory, it's still just a theory, and a single decisive falsification is enough to bring it down. For example, Newtonian mechanics was the going theory in physics for a very long time, and every single experimental observation (along with every single dropped apple!) for a couple hundred years seemed

to confirm it. But experiments in the twentieth century finally brought it down, so to speak, and centuries of "confirmation" weren't enough to save it.

But doesn't this mean that a completely untested theory that someone just made up is as "good" as a long-standing accepted theory, or that there is no reason to prefer the "phase transition" theory of melting ice over the "hidden liquid-demons" theory? We can address these problems by adding that (1) we should prefer simpler theories over theories with unnecessary complications, and (2) we shouldn't even consider theories that aren't falsifiable. Scientific theories take risks; they make claims that can be tested and falsified, and this is why we value scientific theories! Popper said theories that are not falsifiable are "pseudoscience" and should be ignored because they can explain away any seemingly contradictory evidence, so if they are wrong, there's no way we'd ever know.

Popper talked about Marxism as such a theory, and for the sake of balance I'll note that we can say the same thing about libertarianism. In the one case, if the proletariat hasn't risen up, the true believer will say that it's because they're enthralled by the false consciousness of capitalist ideology; in the other, if the free market isn't fixing everything yet, it's because we need yet more tax cuts and yet fewer regulations. In pseudoscience, even evidence that seems to be against the theory is interpreted as confirmation.

Let's look more at Popper's "demarcation" theory, differentiating science from pseudoscience. What kind of evidence would falsify the theory of evolution? Is there any possible kind of fossil that evolutionary biology wouldn't simply treat as (perhaps puzzling) data to be accounted for from within the theory?

What about the theory of intelligent design? Is it any more or any less falsifiable than the theory of evolution?

If you see a difference in falsifiability, is this enough to identify each theory—evolution and intelligent design—as either science or pseudoscience? If not, what other reasons might justify treating one as science and the other as pseudoscience?

IF A SCIENTIFIC THEORY IS UNFALSIFIABLE, DOES THAT MEAN THAT IT'S A MATTER OF FAITH?

Falsifiability may not be enough to distinguish science from pseudoscience. Intelligent design is typically regarded as pseudoscience, since any evidence that seems to go against it can be accounted for from within the theory. For example, some have defended intelligent design by claiming that fossils are a trick by the Devil to draw us away from faith. But what about evolutionary biology? What if we found ancient dinosaur bones along with a modern human skeleton, a saddle, and a bottle of whiskey? Even if carbon testing confirmed that the find required significant revision of our views of evolutionary history, biologists wouldn't just give up on the idea of evolution. If evolutionary theory as a whole can't be falsified, is it just as much a pseudoscience as intelligent design?

It is a significant difference that evolutionary biology makes predictions that can turn out to be false—for example, that there are phylogenetic relationships between "related" species. Genetic testing could easily have falsified many hypotheses about whether species are related, but instead it has usually found the kind of genetic overlap that the theory predicted. Intelligent design, by contrast, is not only unfalsifiable as a whole, but does not clearly even make falsifiable hypotheses.

Imre Lakatos (1922–1974), a Hungarian philosopher of science, gave us another useful distinction. Lakatos said that good research programs are progressive—they expand in scope and precision. Failing research programs degenerate—they get too bound up in defending their core claims to do much but keep up with trying to explain each next bit of challenging evidence. Evolutionary biology clearly has been and still is an expanding research program, whereas intelligent design has done little but try to cover the basics—and even here it does so not by making predictions that can be borne out, but simply by claiming "yes, but it could also have been God!" and looking for similar-seeming biblical passages.

It's looking like we have some pretty good ways of accounting for how scientific theories get better, and how we can distinguish science from pseudoscience. But can science get us to the truth?

Science, it has been claimed, works by inductive reasoning, finding a general truth by seeing it over and over again across many similar cases. Here's an inductive argument about induction: All past scientific theories turned out to be wrong. Therefore, our current theories are almost certainly wrong too. Do you think that argument holds up?

Is there anything fundamentally different about today's theories that would prevent this very consistent historical trend (of being proven wrong) from applying to them?

WHAT ARE THE CHANCES THAT ANYTHING WE BELIEVE IS TRUE?

Do we have good reason to believe that, even though we believe them, our current scientific theories must be wrong? Personally, I am on board for this "pessimistic meta-induction" argument: I think we absolutely should assume that our current theories are wrong, just like all the previous theories. And the same thing can be said of the theories we come up with next, and the theories after that, and so on.

Philosophers like me who hold an *instrumentalist* view of science rather than a *realist* view are okay with this—in our view, scientific theories don't directly discover anything real, but are instead just models that have predictive value. Pessimistic meta-induction is a problem in the realist view because it gives us reason to think that science will never "get it right"; but in the instrumentalist view, this doesn't matter. Science is about prediction anyway, not reality.

We'll look at instrumentalism further in the next entries, but for now, let's consider a couple of other interesting arguments that are similar to pessimistic meta-induction. Most people adopt the religious views of their families, and as far

as we know we don't choose which family to be born into. So this means in effect that most people hold a randomly assigned religious view. Even on the assumption that some current religious view or another is correct, the odds of being born into a family that happens to hold it are very slim, so everyone who holds religious views should conclude that their beliefs are almost certainly wrong.

Swedish philosopher Nick Bostrom (1973–) has made a different but similar argument in favor of the "simulation hypothesis." He says it seems likely that a sufficiently advanced human society will create computer-simulated worlds with virtual persons. With sufficient technological progress, these virtual worlds are likely to be cheap, and therefore plentiful. If you accept these assumptions, then it is reasonable to assume that you are living in a simulation, since given these assumptions there are far more virtual persons than real ones, and very numerous virtual worlds but only one real one. So, based on the odds, it's a safe bet that you're just software running on a machine.

Pessimistic meta-induction asks you to believe two things that are at least in tension with one another: that our current scientific theories are wrong, and that this doesn't mean they aren't the best and most accurate theories we've ever had. Is this a problem for science? What does it mean for scientific practices and beliefs?

Scientific practice constantly tests its assumptions and seeks out new and better theories, whereas religious views don't. What difference does that make for whether these arguments are a problem for religion? What difference does that make for what these arguments mean for religious practices and beliefs?

DOES IT MATTER WHETHER SCIENCE IS EVEN ABOUT TRUTH?

German-Jewish political theorist Hannah Arendt (1906–1975) was struck by how commentators, reacting to the launch of Sputnik in 1957, expressed "relief about the first 'step toward escape from men's imprisonment to the earth.'" She thought we were aimlessly pursuing our self-determination, now trying to escape dependence on Earth the Mother. Next, she thought, we would turn to escaping our *own* nature by changing the human species itself, through what today is called genetic engineering. But for the sake of what, and in what direction, do we wish to escape determination by nature without and our nature within? She was worried that it seemed like it didn't occur to us to even ask.

Arendt thought a basic problem is that we have mistaken know-how for knowledge. In her instrumentalist view, science is just a matter of coming up with models that fit with the math and that have success in accurate prediction of experimental results, and that science makes no attempt to figure out what's real and true. And there's nothing wrong with that, so long as we know that science isn't telling us what's real, but is just telling us how to think about the world so that we can get it to respond in predictable ways. But we've lost sight of this, as we can see today in the way that people often think that if there's doubt about a scientific theory, this means the theory isn't important or worth working with.

The scientific realist view, the view that scientific theories aren't just *instruments* but are supposed to tell us about *reality*, gets really bad when science stops making sense in human terms. Arendt quotes Erwin Schrödinger's view that the concepts of high-energy physics are "not perhaps as meaningless as a 'triangular circle,' but [are] much more so than a 'winged lion.'" Schrödinger is most famous for his thought experiment known now as "Schrödinger's Cat," which he intended to demonstrate that the Copenhagen interpretation of quantum mechanics can't possibly be right, since its observer-dependent collapse of superpositions could result in ridiculous situations, like a cat in a box that is both alive and dead. Today, amazingly, Schrödinger's Cat is taught as an explanation of the theory rather than as an argument against it.

We mistakenly turned to science to tell us the truth, when science just tells us how to get things to work in predictable ways. Then, after we mistook "what works" for "the truth," scientific theories that made the math and experiments work out right stopped making any sense at all in human terms. Rather than coming to terms with the fact that science gives us "know-how" rather than knowledge, and seeking knowledge elsewhere, we just gave up on making sense of the world, and settled on just learning more and more about how to make the world do things. In other words, we are locked into a pursuit of know-how and expansion of human capabilities for change and control, with increasingly little guidance by a search for what's true and real. We are less and less in the habit of asking what is worth caring about and doing, as individuals and as a society, and more and more in the habit of uncritically expanding technology to its very limits.

Why is knowing the truth about reality valuable or important?

What difference do you think it makes whether science is about discovering the nature of reality or, instead, about coming up with models able to make increasingly valuable and accurate predictions?

ARE WE RESPONSIBLE ENOUGH FOR THE POWER SCIENCE HAS GIVEN US?

If Arendt was right that we've gotten stuck in an endless and aimless pursuit of technological power and control, what can we do to get things back under control? Hans Jonas (1903–1993), a friend of Arendt's and also a German-Jewish philosopher, thought we needed a new morality of *humility*.

Jonas began by noting that all of our ideas about morality and responsibility date back to times in human history where our technological abilities were dwarfed by the power of nature. Today, however, science and technology have become so powerful that the choices we make can change nature itself—slowly, through global climate change, or suddenly, as in the worries about genetically modified crops "going native," or questions about whether particle accelerator experiments could create a black hole that would violently compress the planet into a gravitational singularity. The clearest and most pressing example in Jonas's time, during World War II and then the Cold War, might be the catastrophic risks presented by nuclear warfare and nuclear reactor meltdowns, including the possible planet-killing effect of a nuclear winter.

Jonas concluded that we need to develop a new kind of morality to deal with our new scientific and technological abilities. It's difficult for us to predict the effects our actions will have, but in the past human capabilities were limited enough to fit pretty well with our similarly limited foresight. This made it plausible to say that all we're responsible for is trying our best, either by having good intentions (as Kant thought) or by putting together an estimate of the impacts of our actions (as the utilitarians argue). But today the scope, scale, and range of human capabilities is now completely out of proportion with our still very limited foresight and wisdom. Not only that, but we have to deal with entirely new questions because we can do things that we never even thought would be possible. We can decide to eliminate entire species, as we have done with the smallpox virus. Global climate change is destroying entire islands and ecosystems, and we've never thought about whether we owe anything to parts of nature that can't have experiences. We can choose to change elements of what we used to think of as "human nature" through medications, for example by regulating neurotransmitter reuptake, or through gene therapy or genetic engineering.

The responsibility that our own science and technology demand from us seems impossible, especially in our age, when we seem so inclined to distraction and entertainment rather than serious contemplation. And yet it is in this age, when meditative thought is closing down in favor of know-how, that our know-how calls most clearly for meditative thought. In the midst of this time of imbalance, Jonas thought that where we once had humility about how helpless we were before the power of nature, today we must develop humility about how helpless we are to understand the meaning and impact of our own actions.

As we use nonrenewable resources or disrupt otherwise self-sustaining systems, for example by depleting polar ice caps and causing sea levels to rise, we remove resources from people who are not yet born and, therefore, can't defend themselves from us. How could we change our government or our idea of responsibility to try to eliminate this form of "taxation without representation"?

Richard Sylvan (1935–1996) asked you to imagine that, following some form of awful accident or war, you are the last remaining human. In one version of the scenario, there are only two living things left in the world: you and a tree. Assume that you know somehow that, if left on its own, the tree would be able to reproduce itself, but that no self-aware, thinking being will ever exist again after you die. If it amused you to do so, would there be anything wrong with chopping down the tree?

Through biological and pharmaceutical interventions, we are increasingly able to change who we are and remake ourselves in our own image. How can you decide what aspects of your body and mind should be changed, if you want, and what, if anything, is off-limits? How can we make good choices together about the future of the species?

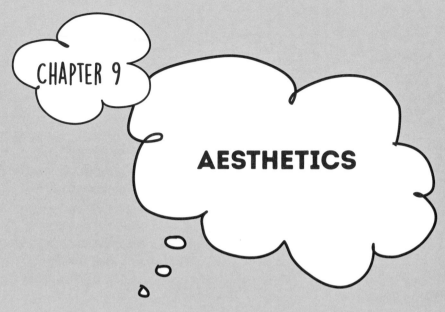

CHAPTER 9

AESTHETICS

The philosophical field of aesthetics includes a number of closely related concerns: our appreciation of the beauty of nature, our appreciation of art, what makes an artwork a great work (or, alternately, crap), the structure and internal logic of art, and what "progress" means in art history. As with the other chapters, there's much more going on in this area of philosophy than we can possibly explore, but we'll get a sampling of issues that will showcase the diversity of questions that we might have about aesthetic experiences.

A quick note: Just as the philosophy of science has focused on physics, perhaps too much, so too has aesthetic theory focused perhaps too much on visual art. I've made sure to address music in particular in these entries for a couple of reasons, including my personal background in music theory and performance. A more important reason, though, is that not everybody goes out of their way to enjoy paintings and performances, but recorded music is part of most people's everyday lives. On the flip side, though, our traditions of playing music have declined, and music has become more of a product and less of an activity than probably at any other time in the history of the species.

IS GREAT ART GREAT EVEN IF YOU DON'T LIKE IT?

It is said that there's no accounting for taste. If someone doesn't care for lobster or Brie cheese, there's not much that can be said to change their opinion. Are we right, though, to say that people who don't like lobster or Brie are in some sense "wrong" in thinking they are not delicious? Surely those with refined palates appreciate these foods, and we would not be likely to choose someone who didn't like them to be a food critic. So there seems to be some basis for thinking that someone who doesn't appreciate fine foods isn't as good a judge of food, even though this puts us in the awkward position of saying sometimes that a dish is excellent even though we might not enjoy it.

We are in the same spot with judgments of taste in art. David Hume's take on this strange situation starts with the observation that, while aesthetic judgment is a matter of personal feeling, our feelings are generally connected in some way to some reality "out there." When you burn your hand, for example, it isn't because you are touching some pain that is there in the fire—the pain is in you, not the fire!—and yet the pain is definitely related to the fire, and if someone else doesn't feel pain when *their* hand is in the fire, you wouldn't be inclined to chalk it up to a difference of opinion.

Now, there's obviously more disagreement about which works of art are great than there is about whether fire hurts, but in Hume's view this is just because aesthetic appreciation is a subtle thing. Pain is about as direct an experience as you can have, but your perception of what is beautiful or moving gets filtered through your personal history, culture, religion, and aesthetic training. We gain refined taste in art through long experience with great art, and through this process we can develop our aesthetic sense and become "true critics." And how do we know which works are great? Well, we listen to those with excellent aesthetic perception, discernment, and judgment, the "true critics." That's circular reasoning, of course, but it's not a problem for refinement of taste. After all, how will you learn to make great food unless you are able to sample and appreciate the wide range and full spectrum of foods and dishes that are most loved and cherished?

How does something get to be judged a great work of art?

Can anything be a great work of art, if enough people say it is?

What if you—or what if everybody—no longer finds a work of art, traditionally recognized as a great work, compelling? Is it still a great work of art?

WHY DO WE FEEL AWE BEFORE NATURE?

Immanuel Kant considered aesthetic experiences, along with the other topics we've already heard about from him. He addressed at least something in almost every area of philosophy—and, amazingly, Kant did all of his important writing quite late in his career, publishing his first great work when he was in his fifties.

One of the topics he considered was the experience of *the sublime*. We don't talk much about the experience of the sublime anymore, but we're certainly familiar with the feeling: an overwhelming feeling of awe that we have standing before the ocean, or a towering cliff, or near the thunder of a waterfall, or in the midst of a near-terrifying violent storm.

In the experience of very large things (the "mathematically sublime"), we have a concept of the whole as a single thing, but we also know that it is made of individual bits. We can comprehend each individual bit and understand what it is in normal terms, but the whole thing is incomprehensibly large if we really think about it. So,

for example, we can understand a bucket of ocean water—how large it is, what could be in it, and so on. When we look at the ocean, we try to extrapolate from that normal understanding of an amount of water to the incomprehensible and overwhelming multitude of bucketfuls of water. We are awed because although we cannot understand how much water there is before us, we are still able to see it and conceptualize it as a whole. Kant thought that it's the way that our conceptual ability outstrips our understanding that produces this feeling of wonder within us.

In experiences of the great force of nature in violent storms or waterfalls (the "dynamically sublime"), we are aware of how unimaginably powerful it is compared to us, and we feel awe in our ability to observe it without fleeing or being destroyed. As with the mathematically sublime, we stand in amazement of our own ability to deal with something on such a massive and overwhelming scale.

We don't usually find water or dirt terribly impressive. Why do we find ourselves enthralled by the Grand Canyon or the ocean? Does Kant's theory of the mathematically sublime fit your experience, or is there something more that needs to be said?

We are in awe, also, of the forces of nature. Why do you think we find it thrilling to stand at the bottom of a powerful waterfall? Does Kant's theory of the dynamically sublime fit your experience, or is there something more that needs to be said? Does Kant's theory fit your experience, or is there something more or something else that needs to be said?

WHAT IS THE EXPERIENCE OF BEAUTY?

Immanuel Kant began his theory of beauty by observing this very unusual dual character of aesthetic judgment: When we say "that is beautiful," we're talking about a feeling we're having, but we're also really making a claim about the thing we're looking at. If others say it's not beautiful, we're inclined to say that they're wrong, but we can't really argue with them because there's nothing we can point to that proves that it's beautiful.

Kant said that the enjoyment that we call "beauty" is found in the free play of our cognitive abilities. (I think this theory works best and makes the most sense if you think of a painting or a symphony.) The thing that we call "beautiful" has a rule-like structure but does not actually follow any strict and definable rules. No matter how complicated and intricate, no recipe can be given for how to make a work of art. The process of experiencing possible patterns emerge and depart, the play of order and meaning within something not determined by order or meaning, is what gives us the pleasure we call beauty. We might say today that beauty appears at the border of structure and chaos.

So, while the experience of beauty is just a feeling, it is based on an interaction between the beautiful object and the basic structures of human thought and understanding. Because those structures of the mind are universal, it makes some sense to claim that others ought to agree with us. This also explains how both things can be true: Beauty is a personal feeling, but the judgment that an object is beautiful still really does identify something about the object, not just our merely personal reaction to it.

It's a surprisingly tidy solution to this apparent conceptual contradiction, but can it account for modern art? But then, maybe our reaction to and appreciation of modernist compositions is more complicated than just finding them "beautiful."

Look up some music from around Kant's time, like Haydn, Mozart, or Beethoven. How well does his theory work for this experience? Do you feel the "free play" in your perception of how structures emerge and change?

Look up *The Duino Elegies* by Rainer Maria Rilke. Read one of them carefully. How well does Kant's theory of beauty fit with your experience?

Look up an image of a painting by Piet Mondrian on the biggest, highest-quality screen you can. Spend five minutes with it. How well does Kant's theory of beauty fit with your experience?

WHY DO WE ENJOY ART?

Do you remember Arthur Schopenhauer, the guy we discussed at the end of Chapter 6, whose theory was that the world is a manifestation of will that survives death? Schopenhauer played the flute. This has been a point of contention among some commentators, most notably Friedrich Nietzsche, who asked how someone can claim that life is suffering and that all the evidence suggests that humanity is some sort of mistake and then have a nice time playing the flute in the evenings? It's not an unreasonable question, but Schopenhauer's account of music helps us see why he, at least, didn't see any conflict between his beliefs and his practice.

Art, in Schopenhauer's view, is a way to express the will so that it becomes external and available for contemplation. When we are able to observe the will in the artwork, separate from us, we are given a momentary rest from being driven by our own will and desires, and this rest is the pleasure that we take in art. By undergoing the movement of the will's struggle and suffering and momentary relief in the proxy of the artwork, our own wills are quieted. We thus supplant the futile strivings and petty dramas of our own wills with a peaceful contemplation of the will, bare and separated from our own desires, in the work of art.

Music, Schopenhauer thought, was the purest art form, representing the will most directly. Other art forms are cluttered up by words, concepts, symbols, and images, but music is nothing but the movements of the will expressed in sound. While the proper goal in life is a negation of the will and a destruction of desire, music is able to give us temporary distance from our own will and, for a moment at least, free us from the vain striving and meaningless hustle and bustle that constitutes life.

There's a story that Mozart once refused to get out of bed to receive a visitor. The man who had come calling went to the piano and loudly played a chord progression, ending on the dominant chord. Mozart, as predicted, couldn't stand it, and had to get up to play the tonic chord and resolve the tension by completing the chord progression. What is it like to experience dissonance as "tension," and why do we enjoy the movement from dissonance to consonance?

What is "harmonious" about musical harmony?

WHAT IS A MELODY?

Hearing a melody seems like a simple thing, but the conditions necessary to have this experience are actually really complicated. When you hear a melody you are hearing isolated notes in succession, but you experience the melody rather than the notes; you hear them as connected to and part of each other, even though you only hear one at a time! The French phenomenologist Maurice Merleau-Ponty (1908–1961) compared a melody to a film. In the film, what we literally perceive are only isolated pictures, each of which is gone before the next arrives, and yet we experience only movement and change and not any of the images as images. In the same way, in listening to a melody, we experience the *gestalt*, or the system of elements as a system, and experience the elements within the melody only as parts of what we hear essentially as a whole.

Each note is experienced in the context of the notes that come before, but not as a kind of remembering. As Merleau-Ponty pointed out, if we remembered the previous notes, we would be recalling something. Instead, we continue to feel the previous notes even though we are no longer (literally) hearing them. Another phenomenologist, Edmund Husserl (1859–1938), called this *retention*. The experience of the previous note is *retained* in our current experience of the current note, and the note we hear is heard against the background of those notes we *retain* (the notes that we no longer hear, but which we continue to feel rather than merely remember).

Husserl pointed out that there's also a similar process of *protention*, where we "feel" the notes that we have not yet heard but which are implied in the note we currently hear—this is what got Mozart out of bed in the story in the previous entry. The melody emerges from the notes we hear placed against the notes we *retain*, and containing the notes we *protain*.

That's a lot of work to explain hearing a melody! Why did philosophers spend so much time on this? Phenomenologists are philosophers of experience who try to figure out what's actually happening in our experiences and what isn't. This can help us learn all kinds of things that are otherwise really hard to figure out. In this case, we find out that a melody is an experience constituted by a blurred mix of our past, our present, and our possible futures, and that gives us insight into how inaccurate it is to think that there is a single and clear present moment in experience, or that the perceptions of the senses are simple, clear, and factual.

Think for a minute about this sentence. At the beginning is an imperative verb ("Think"), where the subject (you!) is implied. The following words "for a minute" modify the thinking that you're supposed to do, and then the "about" tells you that the object of the thinking will finally arrive. And then there it is, "this sentence," and that lets you close out the open possibilities of what you were being asked to think about from the first word. Do you see how retention and protention work in reading and listening to sentences? How is it different from how these processes work in listening to music?

Look up an abstract painting—if you don't have a work or artist that comes to mind, I'll recommend finding something by Paul Klee. Spend some time with the image on the largest, highest-resolution screen you can find. Think about how your eyes move and your focus shifts. Do you think protention and retention are at work in your experience of this painting?

HOW MUCH OF LISTENING IS REALLY FASHION?

German-Jewish philosopher Theodor Adorno (1903–1969) wrote deep and complex analyses of popular culture, focusing most of all on music. In an influential essay, "On the Fetish-Character in Music and the Regression of Listening," he claimed that our engagement with music is characterized, on the one hand, by encountering music as a commodity, and on the other hand as an element of personal identity and comfort. (Here he was speaking about regression and repetition in the Freudian sense, where, like children, we demand the same thing over and over again.) Notably missing in both these elements is the actual aesthetic experience of the music!

The commodity character of music is revealed in a number of ways. In Classical music, orchestras perform only particular famous pieces, because they are the ones that everyone knows—because they are the ones that orchestras perform—and a great many works at least as valuable are almost entirely ignored. Adorno wrote about how the consumer displays the tickets proudly, showing that his concern is having acquired the cachet and social meaning of having had the experience, not the experience itself.

In popular music, style and fashion form the basis of our experience. Adorno wrote that our rage against music that isn't up-to-date, that has become "corny," shows that our previous "enjoyment" of this music was only a pseudopleasure of consumption and amusement rather than a real aesthetic pleasure. Today we can easily imagine he would say that our musical consumption is as much about what is associated with our preferred styles of clothes and makeup as it is about what we might otherwise prefer to listen to.

Adorno didn't discuss our attachment to the musical styles of our youth, but it fits in perfectly with his analysis—he might have said that we form a lasting attachment to this music because it has become bound up with our self-identity and serves as a safe memory to which we can retreat at moments of uncertainty, freeing ourselves from the burden of experiencing change and growth. Hearing it gives us the empty calories of musical macaroni and cheese. In these ways, we see that listening today has little to do with music.

Chances are we'd be judgey about someone who, today, listens pretty much exclusively to 1970s disco, 1980s new wave, or 1990s neo-swing. What does it say about our relationship with music that music can become embarrassing?

Do you listen to new and emerging artists in your preferred genres of music? *If not*, go get a sense of who's who among new artists and make them your music for this week. *If so*, figure out what music was like in your preferred genres five or ten years earlier than the oldest music in the genre that you know well, and make that your music for this week. At the end of the week, reflect on what you found challenging and what you learned about your relationship to music.

WHAT IS ART?

In his theory of artistic progress, American philosopher Arthur Danto (1924–2013) adopted a general view of the progress of art from German philosopher G.W.F. Hegel (1770–1831) and used it to provide a detailed analysis of modern and postmodern art. In Hegel's original theory, art has progressed through different eras, very roughly speaking, by a gradual decrease of concrete and imitative elements in art and an increase in the expressive and conceptual elements. In Greek sculpture, the statue is viewed as the god itself, and serves a symbolic function. In Classical art, most clearly in painting, realistic and literal representation is combined with expressive content, properly reflecting in beauty the nature of humanity as both free and material. In Romantic art, most clearly in poetry and music, the inner nature of humanity is emphasized. In Hegel's view, art is *about* the representation of humanity, and so symbolic art is not yet art, whereas Romantic art represents a disintegration of art from its Classical realization.

Danto extended and changed this historical view, and his version is much less abstract and much more plausible. In his view, art progresses by breaking apart the limits of what can be art. At first art was imitative and took on an expressive function. The imitative aspects of art were broken down, and art became that process by which we see that each stylistic and conventional constraint on what "counts" as art is in fact unnecessary to art.

I'll show you what I mean. In Impressionism, the actual presence of the paint comes forward in the viewer's experience of the work, de-emphasizing the importance of representation. In Modernism and Abstract Expressionism, the process is carried further. In found art, the process of artistic creation itself is shown to be unnecessary. Today, according to Danto, we are "after the end of art," because art, understood as this process of breaking down its own constraints, has finished. Today, it seems, there are no rules about what "counts," except that art must be a further development and what used to be art cannot be art today.

In 1917, Marcel Duchamp (1887–1968) submitted a urinal to an art exhibition, and signed it "R. Mutt."

In 1921, Alexander Rodchenko (1891–1956) produced a series of three paintings. One panel was red. Another was yellow. The third was blue.

In 1964, Andy Warhol (1928–1987) silkscreened a wood block to look like a box of Brillo brand soap pads.

In 1971, Chris Burden (1946–2015) performed a piece entitled "Shoot," in which he had someone shoot him in the arm.

In 1991, Damien Hirst (1965–) produced a work, "The Physical Impossibility of Death in the Mind of Someone Living," which consisted of a fourteen-foot tiger shark in formaldehyde.

CHAPTER 10

DEATH

Chapter 7 stated that every entry in the book, at its base, is really about questions of knowledge and reality. That's certainly true when we speak of the "basis" of philosophical questions in an abstract, conceptual sense, but if we speak of the basis of philosophical inquiry in practical experience instead, a case can be made that it is death that forms the basis of every question in the book.

Some questions, like those about God, can be traced back to a fear of death and its meaning. Science and the quest for knowledge can be viewed as an attempt to control and predict the world, perhaps a kind of sublimation of our impossible desire to control and predict our departure from the world. Questions of how to live—whether related to happiness, justice, morality, or art—gain their force from our awareness that we only seem to get the opportunity to do so once, so we'd better get it right while we can.

SHOULD WE FEAR DEATH?

Socrates's death is almost certainly the most famous death in the history of philosophy. In 399 B.C.E., after he was found guilty of impiety and being a corrupter of the youth, the prosecution asked for the death penalty. According to the structure of trials in ancient Athens, the defense was able to propose an alternate sentence and the jury would decide between the two proposed sentences. Socrates showed a surprising lack of concern for his fate, proposing that he be sentenced to free meals in the Prytaneum, an honor usually given to Olympic victors. (He did backpedal a bit, and eventually offered to pay a fine of 30 *minae*, estimated to be equivalent to around $40,000 in today's dollars.) The jury chose the sentence of death—and did so by a wider margin than they had chosen the verdict of guilty! In explaining his lack of concern for his life, Socrates said that he had been given by the gods to Athens as a gadfly, to awaken the city into wakefulness through his constant biting inquiry. And so to agree to stop his challenging and questioning or to promise to leave town (exile is probably the alternate sentence that the jury was expecting from him) would amount to deserting his post, and, like a virtuous soldier, he would rather face death by staying at his post than flee out of fear for his life.

He also said that people say that death is either nothingness or a migration of the soul. In the first case, then to die is to enter a sleepless dream, which he said is a pleasant thing. In the second case, then to die is to have the opportunity in the afterlife to speak with the greatest of men: Orpheus! Hesiod! Homer! He ended his address by saying, "The hour of departure has arrived, and we go our separate ways, I to die, and you to live. Which of these two is better only God knows."

What do you believe happens to you after death—or at least, what's your working hypothesis?

Are you afraid of death? Why or why not?

WHAT IS WRONG ABOUT ENDING YOUR LIFE?

David Hume published on many controversial topics. His comments on religion were controversial enough to make him lose out on positions at the University of Edinburgh and the University of Glasgow, and to nearly be tried for heresy by the Church of Scotland. Suicide, though, was such a dangerous topic to address that Hume left his essay on the topic to be published only after his death. In England at the time, suicide was so looked down upon that those who were found guilty of it were not allowed to be buried in the same graveyards as others, were buried at night without mourners, and had their property seized by the state rather than being passed down through inheritance.

Hume began his consideration by claiming that if suicide is a crime, it must be a crime against God, against our neighbors, or against ourselves. The first option is most commonly discussed today as the idea that only God should decide the hour of our deaths. Hume reasoned that God established various limits on our behaviors and actions, yet certainly made it possible for us to end our lives. But are we perhaps upsetting the course of events established by God in accordance with His plan? If God's plan includes our choices, Hume reasoned, then this can't be the case—and, we might add, if God's plan doesn't include our choices, then we are as surely going against His will if we save someone's life, and we don't regard that as wrong.

As to our duties to our neighbors, we can note that we surely have a duty to give back to a society that supports us. But we don't think there's anything wrong with becoming a hermit, and the hermit no longer contributes to society, but doesn't depend on society either, and so owes nothing to it. Suicide is no different than becoming a hermit, in this respect.

Finally, regarding our duty to ourselves, Hume said, "I believe that no man ever threw away life, while it was worth keeping. For such is our natural horror of death, that small motives will never be able to reconcile us to it." And so, we can be assured that anyone who chooses suicide chooses it for significant reasons and based on serious interests.

Suppose that someone, not depressed, but in pain and facing unavoidable deterioration from an incurable disease, wishes to die. What considerations might make their choice morally wrong?

Suppose the person in the previous question needs help to end their life. Assuming for the moment that it would be acceptable for them to do so on their own, would there be anything wrong with assisting in the process?

What if they are not depressed, not in pain, and not facing disease, but are simply weary of living? What does this change, if anything?

WHEN IS WAR JUSTIFIED?

Just war theory has a long tradition, going back at least to St. Thomas Aquinas and St. Augustine. Traditionally, these are the conditions that have been viewed as necessary for a just declaration of war:

- That there be a just cause, based on a country's aggression against another nation or against its own people
- That all other options in halting that aggression, short of war, have been exhausted
- That there be a fair chance of success (for otherwise war would only be a useless shedding of additional blood)
- That the good that would come from military success outweigh the harms created by the war itself

The first and second Iraq wars provide good, contrasting examples. From this traditional view of just war, the first Iraq war seems quite justifiable: Iraq's invasion of Kuwait was obviously an aggressive act, and there were clear reasons to take military action immediately in defense of a sovereign nation. (Of course, Iraq was a sovereign nation as well, but in just war theory, a state that engages in military aggression loses its right to be left alone.)

The second Iraq war is much more troubling, because it was not justified by an act of aggression. It is true that Iraq had "waged war" on its own people, especially the Kurds, but the war was not justified by appeal to this valid reason for humanitarian intervention—instead, the idea that Iraq was developing weapons of mass destruction was used as a justification.

This argument for a right to wage preemptive war is deeply troubling for just war theory. Michael Walzer (1935–), probably the most prominent just war theorist today, argues that preventative war is justified only when a country has made both hostile declarations and concrete preparations for war. The idea of going to war to prevent a state from even *becoming* a threat in the first place, however, seems very unjust—there are other options short of war (for example, sanctions) if there has been no act of aggression, and the evils prevented by the war are uncertain, whereas the harms of going to war are significant and certain.

Today, a new challenge is to figure out where cyberwarfare fits in. The Stuxnet worm, computer malware purportedly developed by the US and Israeli governments, for example, seriously set back Iran's ability to develop nuclear weapons through preemptive action, but it did so without causing bloodshed. Was this a troubling preemptive strike, or a preferable action short of war to defuse the situation?

Is war justified to prevent a country that has declared itself to be our enemy from becoming a threat? (That is, assuming that the country is not currently a threat.)

Is cyberwarfare subject to conditions similar to traditional just war conditions? What, if anything, needs to be changed when cyberwarfare is being considered?

CAN PREPARING FOR WAR BE A PATH TO PEACE?

In the abstract, preemptive war does seem clearly unjust. The enemy is not a threat and may not ever become one. Such a war violates the sovereignty of a nation that has taken no aggressive action. The doctrine of preemption undermines international peace, because it seems to offer a blanket justification for any nation to wage war against any other nation with a stated hostility to another nation—it would justify any ally of Iran or Israel in attacking the other on the basis of their often-stated hostility. And what about India or Pakistan or their allies? Or the United States or North Korea? But the extreme threat posed by weapons of mass destruction seems to many to be sufficient reason to say that a doctrine of preemption is *necessary* today, even if it can't be morally justified.

Immanuel Kant's view on war was as strict as his view on lying. Any kind of aggression, including aggressive stances short of war, is unacceptable in his view. Even simply maintaining a standing army, he argued, leads toward war and is unacceptable. If a neighboring nation has a large military, we feel we need a large military as well, just in case that neighbor *becomes* hostile one day. Of course, they will inevitably start to feel the same way about our military, and an arms race quickly begins between two nations, even if neither is hostile. Eventually, the logic of preemption just seems to *demand* waging war: Attack the other (nonhostile) nation before it becomes too strong to resist (if it became hostile).

Kant admitted that it seems unrealistic to say that we should not keep ourselves ready to defend ourselves. But, he said, the reality is the other way around: It is unrealistic to think that preparing for war will bring peace. It is true that a country that does not prepare for war makes itself vulnerable, but it is also true that the only way we will ever have peace is for all nations to refuse to prepare for war. The high road, in this case, is the only road that leads to the desired destination: perpetual peace.

Assume for the moment that Iraq actually had been developing weapons of mass destruction in 2003. Given the massive destructive force of WMDs, would going to war against Saddam Hussein's regime have been the right choice, even if it was unjust?

Do you think deterrence of war through building and maintaining a strong military is a good path to peace? Why or why not?

IF EVERYTHING ENDS, DOES THAT MAKE IT MATTER LESS?

In his 1873 essay "On Truth and Lies in a Nonmoral Sense," Friedrich Nietzsche wrote:

Once upon a time, in some out of the way corner of that universe which is dispersed into numberless twinkling solar systems, there was a star upon which clever beasts invented knowing. That was the most arrogant and mendacious minute of "world history," but nevertheless, it was only a minute. After nature had drawn a few breaths, the star cooled and congealed, and the clever beasts had to die.

One might invent such a fable, and yet he still would not have adequately illustrated how miserable, how shadowy and transient, how aimless and arbitrary the human intellect looks within nature. There were eternities during which it did not exist. And when it is all over with the human intellect, nothing will have happened.

Sigmund Freud (1856–1939) wrote a commentary on death and meaning, very closely connected to this little story from Nietzsche. Now, we don't usually think of Freud as a philosopher, but he admitted that Nietzsche was an early influence on him (although he didn't admit the full range of that influence), and he even quoted Schopenhauer.

In this 1915 essay, called "On Transience," Freud recalled a conversation with a young poet, during a walk through the countryside. Freud doesn't name him, but there's reason to believe that this poet was Rainer Maria Rilke (1875–1926), and his stunningly beautiful and achingly tragic poetry would make him fit the poet's role in the story well. The poet's enjoyment of the countryside was prevented by his thought that it was transient; that winter would soon bring death upon its lush splendor and cease its futile exuberance.

Freud wrote that the "proneness to decay of all that is beautiful and perfect" drives us either to the despondence of this poet or to "wish fulfillment" in the refusal to believe that death is the end. Using what is called a "hermeneutics of suspicion," Freud stated that the belief in the immortal soul is too much in line with our desires to think that our tendency to believe in it could be based in anything but our own desires. It is too convenient an answer to be convincing. But Freud also rejected the poet's withdrawal from emotional attachment to a world of merely fleeting beauty. Transience does not destroy value, but should *intensify* it, as the scarcity of a good usually does. As he wrote, "a flower that blossoms only for a single night does not seem to us on that account less lovely."

Freud speculated that the poet is mourning in advance for what will be lost, making every attachment and enjoyment painful, due to the knowledge that the object of this appreciation and admiration is doomed to pass away. As Freud wrote about elsewhere, after making an emotional investment in someone, when the beloved dies, the world seems impoverished, because the value placed in them through your love is then missing from the world. Mourning, the process of letting go of the lost and beginning to reinvest value in the world, is painful and difficult, but ceasing to make these attachments in the first place is a poor solution, and mourning in advance only extends the pain and robs us of joy.

Freud wrote this shortly after the end of the Great War, now, tragically, known as World War I. In the Great War, European nations descended again into hideous and inhumane bloodshed of a kind that they had thought was a thing of the past, and Freud himself went through a kind of mourning for the loss of his illusion that these nations were civilized. It seems he wrote his essay on transience to reflect on this. Even though World War I showed how fragile and temporary, how transient the achievements of civilization and progress in human morality and rational action are, still, this should not be a cause for depression or hopelessness. Rather it is a reason to value these cultural achievements all the more highly, and to continue to work toward them.

We may perhaps say the same thing of this brief flicker of thought and meaning within a universe whose farthest reaches in time and space seem to contain only emptiness. Such a rare and fleeting flower, so beautiful and so temporary it makes one cry.

Not just us, today—although that's true as well—but all living beings able to think and care will die. Not only individually, but it seems as a whole as well; eventually the earth itself will be rendered sterile and barren, leaving unimaginable eons of nothing but dead rocks floating in the empty vacuum of space, far outweighing this fleeting moment where self-awareness and meaning flickered briefly in the cold and eternal night.

You might ask what the point of doing anything might be, since this moment is so isolated and temporary, surrounded by endless meaningless emptiness before or after. But instead of letting that darkness extinguish this light, can you see how to let that darkness make this light brighter? Whatever happens in the future, every person, every moment, every choice we have is here and full and complete right now. Every one. What does it mean to you to let the coming winter bring greater joy to the spring?

INDEX

ABOUT THE AUTHOR

D.E. Wittkower, PhD, is a professor and the chair of philosophy and religious studies at Old Dominion University in Norfolk, Virginia. A specialist in philosophy of technology, he researches and teaches on information ethics, cybersecurity, and the conduct of everyday life through digital mediation. In addition to being editor in chief of the *Journal of Sociotechnical Critique*, he is editor or author of seven books on philosophy for a general audience, and author or coauthor of around fifty academic book chapters and journal articles. He has also written for *Slate*, *Speakeasy*, and *Passcode*, and has recorded a dozen audiobooks with LibriVox that, combined, have been accessed over a million times. In his spare time he is an award-winning orchid grower, restores vintage fountain pens that he sells on Etsy at DWittRestoration, and fences foil competitively. He lives by the Chesapeake Bay in Norfolk, Virginia, with his wife, two children, and four cats. Continue the conversation on TikTok @d.e.wittkower.